Our Supernatural

PRAYER
LANGUAGE
TONGUES

By Dr. Alan Pateman

1. *The Reality of a Warrior*

2. *Healing and Deliverance, A Present Reality*

3. *Control, A Powerful Force*

4. *His Life is in the Blood*

5. *Sexual Madness, In a Sexually Confused World (co-authored with Jennifer Pateman)*

6. *Apostles, Can the Church Survive Without Them?*

7. *Prayer, Ingredients for Successful Intercession, Part One*

8. *Prayer, Touching the Heart of God, Part Two*

9. *The Early Years, Anointed Generals Past and Present, Part One of Four*

10. *Revival Fires, Anointed Generals Past and Present, Part Two of Four*

11. *Why War, A Biblical Approach to the Armour of God and Spiritual Warfare*

12. *Forgiveness, the Key to Revival*

13. *His Faith, Positions us for Possession*

14. *Seduction & Control: Infiltrating Society and the Church*

15. *Kingdom Management for Anointed Prosperity*

16. *TONGUES, our Supernatural Prayer Language*

17. *Seven Pillars for Life and Kingdom Prosperity*

18. *WINNING by Mastering your Mind*

19. *Laying Foundations*

20. *Apostles and the Local Church*

21. *Preparations for Ministry*

22. *Developments and Provision*

23. *The Age of Apostolic Apostleship*

BY DR. JENNIFER PATEMAN

AVAILABLE FROM APMI PUBLICATIONS, AMAZON.COM AND OTHER RETAIL OUTLETS

Our Supernatural

PRAYER
LANGUAGE
TONGUES

DR. ALAN PATEMAN

BOOK TITLE:
Tongues, our Supernatural Prayer Language

WRITTEN BY Dr. ALAN PATEMAN
ISBN: 978-1-909132-44-3
eBook ISBN: 978-1-909132-45-0

Published By:
APMI Publications
In Partnership with Truth for the Journey Books **16**
Email: publications@alanpateman.com
www.AlanPatemanMinistries.com

Acknowledgements:
Author/Design/Senior Editor/Publisher: Apostle Dr. Alan Pateman
Editing/Proofreading/Research: Dr. Jennifer Pateman
Computer Administration/Office Manager: Dr. Dorothea Struhlik

Unless otherwise indicated, all scriptural quotations are from the HOLY BIBLE, NEW INTERNATIONAL VERSION ®. NIV ®. Copyright © 1973, 1978, 1984 by the International Bible Society. Used by permission of Zondervan Publishing House. All rights reserved.

*Where scriptures appear with special emphasis (**in bold**, italic or <u>underlined</u>) we have edited them ourselves in order to bring focused attention within the context of this subject being taught.*

❖

Dedication

To all those who need to have their battery recharged.

❖

Table of Contents

❖

Foreword

The Pentecostal Century

We cannot look into this subject without first sharing a snapshot of where it all began in regards to Church history.

So what about the last hundred years? Although we are in the 21st century and don't want to go backwards to go forwards, it's helpful to know where we've been, to help us know where we're going!

So let's consider some important events that have helped forge a significant handprint on the past, as far as church history is concerned, and how that relates to us today.

We start the journey with Agnes Ozman of all people, whose marginal insignificance became *remarkably significant* in the greater scheme of things! Let me explain: on January 1st 1901, (which incidentally marked the first day of the 20th century), this seemingly irrelevant young lady was baptised in the Holy Spirit.

What's so monumental?

Well this event helped change history, as we know it. Ozman was part of a small bible school in Topeka Kansas, which was led by Charles Fox Parham, (aka Father of Pentecost).

Her glorious experience, (the manifestation of the gift of tongues) meant that she became the first pentecostal of the 20th century! A tall statement perhaps, but according to J. Roswell Flower, the founding secretary of the Assemblies of God, Ozman's experience was the *"the touch felt round the world,"* and was such a significant event that it helped birth the Pentecostal-Charismatic-Movement and brought one of the mightiest revivals and missionary movements in church history.

In short, the prelude for this was that Parham had given all of his students an assignment to study the book of Acts and the bible's evidence of the baptism in the Holy Spirit. Each student was given three days to fulfil the task.

On the final day of the assignment, and to his astonishment, Parham discovered that each student came to the same conclusion. That although there were different manifestations of the Spirit occurring during the outpouring of Pentecost, *every* **recipient baptised by the Holy Spirit spoke in other tongues, without exception.**

The scripture below shows how **ALL** were included:

*When the day of Pentecost was fully come, **they were ALL with one accord in one place.** And suddenly there came a sound from heaven as of a rushing mighty wind, and **it filled ALL the house** where they were sitting.*

*And there appeared unto them cloven tongues like as of fire, and **it sat upon EACH of them.** And they were **ALL filled with the Holy Ghost, and begun to speak with other tongues,** as the Spirit gave them utterance.*

(Acts 2:1-4 KJV)

Equipped with Power

This assignment had stirred the hearts of these students and during the following evening meeting, Angus Ozman asked Charles Parham to lay hands on her, so that she might receive the baptism of the Holy Spirit. Ozman believed she was called to the mission field and wanted to be equipped with spiritual power.

"Only tongues set on fire by the Holy Spirit can witness the saving power of Christ with power to save others" (Bounds 280).

Initially hesitating, in front of 75 other people in the room, Parham admitted to her that he didn't speak in other tongues himself! Nevertheless he laid hands on her and prayed.

Recalling events afterwards he said, "I had scarcely repeated three dozen sentences when a glory fell upon her, a halo seemed to surround her head and face, and she began speaking in the Chinese language, and was unable to speak in English for three days" (Goff 66-67).

Not long after her experience Parham was also released in other tongues: "There came a slight twist in my throat, a glory fell over me and I began to worship God in a Swedish tongue, which later changed to other languages and continued..." (Parham 5)

January 21st, 1901

Successively, Parham's first message was all about the experience of baptism in the Holy Spirit, with the evidence of speaking in other tongues. This was now to be Parham's life message.

His life culminated at the age of 56 (in 1929) and since then this worldwide Pentecostal-Charismatic-Movement has marched forwards to unfathomable heights.

Millions of pentecostals now exist today, because of one revelation that - everyone should be speaking in tongues – and be living the deeper life of the Spirit and not the flesh.

What a humble beginning for such a worldwide movement that steadily became the largest Christian movement of the 20th century; beginning with just a handful of students (in January 1901).

Today pentecostalism - in the 21st century - continues to flourish globally, with staggering numbers well into the hundreds of millions! And it took the likes of Charles Fox Parham (and others) to cause some historians to refer to the 20th century as the **"Pentecostal Century."**

❖

Introduction

Building a Spiritual or Natural House?

God's building us up to be a *spiritual* house: *"Ye also, <u>as lively stones, are built up a spiritual house</u>, a holy priesthood, to offer up spiritual sacrifices, acceptable to God by Jesus Christ"* (*1 Peter 2:4-5 KJV*).

> *Like living stones,* **let yourselves be assembled into a spiritual house...**
>
> (1 Peter 2:5 VOICE)

If we don't amount to a "spiritual house" then what are we? God wants us to be spiritual. "God is a Spirit" and according to John 4:24, He "must" be worshipped "in spirit and in truth."

So then, does praying in the prayer language of the Spirit, make us more authentic as Christians? No. That's not the point. The point is this: if Jude 20 clearly reveals that praying in the Spirit builds us up, it's in our interest not to ignore it!

Evangelical or Pentecostal?

I often ask church members wherever I go, if they can locate themselves, as being either evangelical or pentecostal. Some members are confused as to who they are supposed to be!

Either is good but this is the question I'm really asking: **"Are you part of a spiritual house, where living water is flowing or are you part of a natural house, that's just developed into a religious club?"**

Let's look at the difference:

- **Pentecostal:** derived from Pentecost (Acts 2). Emphasis: on the authority of God's Word and the necessity of accepting Christ as personal Lord and Saviour, including the baptism with the Holy Spirit (with evidence of speaking in tongues). Christians are to live a Spirit–filled and empowered life (including operating in spiritual gifts).

- **Evangelical:** salvation by grace through faith in Jesus Christ. Emphasis: on the authority of God's Word, salvation (the born-again experience), and sharing the salvation message (evangelism).

- **The Charismatic Movement:** developed from pentecostalism, where pentecostal beliefs began penetrating the norm and were adopted by the mainline protestant denominations (including the Catholic Church!) Emphasis: again shared with pentecostals (especially the work of the Holy Spirit, spiritual gifts, and miracles) but remained part of a mainline church (renewal). Difference: charismatics are more likely than pentecostals to believe that tongues are not a necessary evidence of the baptism of the Holy Spirit.

The Pentecostal River is Always Flowing

Being truly "pentecostal," in context with Acts 2, is not just about conversion but living in overcoming power! In her book "Breaking Free - Discover the Victory of Total Surrender," Beth Moore says, "We can be saved, the Holy Spirit can dwell in us, and yet we can continually live in defeat because **the enemy can outwit us if we do not depend on the Holy Spirit** and the Word of God" (Moore 18).

The Holy Spirit must be manifest through our lives and His living water (tongues) must continually flow up out of us like a river, building us up inwardly so that our spirit man is stronger than our outward man. Only an *empowered life* can bring glory to His name!

This river of life flows from deep within, as Psalm 42:7 tells us, "Deep calls to deep." Additionally, in the Voice translation of the bible, Isaiah 59:19 says of the Holy Spirit that, "He will come on like a torrential flood…" And Jesus told us that if we drink from Him we'd "never thirst again" (John 4:13-14 VOICE). He also spoke of rivers of living water flowing from within our being:

*If any of you is thirsty, come to Me and drink. If you believe in Me, the Hebrew Scriptures say that **rivers of living water will flow from within you.** Jesus was referring to the **realities of life in the Spirit** made available to everyone who believes in Him. But the Spirit had not yet arrived because Jesus had not been glorified.*

(John 7:37-39 VOICE)

Once again it's crucial that we locate ourselves, both individually and corporately. What kind of house is being built (natural or spiritual) and is the RIVER flowing?

Truly Seeing and Hearing God

As ever there is a balance to everything. So here I want to quote Rick Joyner as he points out, that we must see God as He is, not as we reduce Him to be. As Jesus will deliberately do the unfamiliar, unexpected and unpredictable in our lives!

Rick says, "If we are going to walk as He walked, we too must learn to see and hear as He did. This is the great lesson of the two men on the road to Emmaus. The resurrected Christ appeared to these disciples and preached to them about Himself for quite awhile.

*Afterward Jesus appeared in a **different form** to two of them while they were walking in the country. These returned and reported it to the rest; but they did not believe them either.*

(Mark 16:12)

This was Christ preaching Christ - it will never be more anointed than that! Yet they still could not recognise Him. Why? Because **'He appeared in a different form.'"**

18

Note: the Greek word for "form" *morphē* means: *"external appearance" (see Strong's G3444).* So did Jesus transform His outward appearance just by dressing differently than they'd seen Him before?

Either way, after hours of walking and talking together (approx. seven miles distance), it was only as they heard Him praying, that they finally recognised Him. Yet in Luke 24:16 it says that while they were still on the road, "they were *kept* from recognizing him." Why?

Recognising Jesus

Rick Joyner explains this, "One of the primary reasons why we miss the Lord when He tries to draw near to us is because **we tend to know the Lord according to a** *form* **rather than by the** *Spirit.*

If we are Charismatics, we tend to only recognise Him when He comes to us through a Charismatic. If we are a Baptist, we tend to only know Him when He comes to us through a Baptist.

However, He will usually approach us in a *form* that is different from what we are used to. He did so with His own disciples after His resurrection. **This is because He is always seeking for us to <u>know Him through the Spirit</u>, <u>not through externals</u>"** (Joyner, Overcoming Evil in the Last Days 23-24).

Developing a Spiritual Appetite

In his book "The Supernatural Power of a Transformed Mind" Bill Johnson writes, "I have come to see that the normal Christian life means miracles, spiritual intervention, and revelation. It means peace, joy, love, a sense of well-being and purpose - all these traits that elude so many Christians.

Written into the spiritual DNA of every believer is an appetite for the impossible... The Holy Spirit, the very Spirit who raised Jesus from the dead, lives in us, making it impossible for us to be content...

Our hearts know there is much more to life than what we perceive with our senses; we are spiritually agitated by the lack of connection with the realm of the supernatural.

In the end, nothing satisfies the heart of the Christian like seeing so-called impossibilities bow their knees to the name of Jesus. **Anything less than this is abnormal and unfulfilling...**

We live in an unprecedented hour where people are hungering for and stepping into their destiny in great numbers, fulfilling the purpose of God for mankind on earth. It's an amazing, unprecedented time to be alive, and you and I get to be part of it!" (Johnson, Bill, The Supernatural Power of a Transformed Mind 28)

Receiving the Fullness

Precious reader have you ever received the baptism of the Holy Spirit with the evidence of speaking in tongues?

If not, then let's pray:

Heavenly Father, I am your child because I believe in the death, burial and resurrection of Jesus Christ. You so loved the world that You gave Your one and only son, so that I could have eternal life.

I believe that He came in the flesh to die for my sins and to pay the ransom in full, so that I could be reconciled back to You Father.

As my Lord and Saviour Jesus taught, **"How much more shall your heavenly Father give the Holy Spirit to those who ask Him?"** *(Luke 11:13 KJV)*

Trusting what He said, I believe that you are both able and willing and won't hesitate to answer my prayer. So I ask You right now to fill me - spirit, soul and body - to overflowing, with your Holy Spirit!

I want Your fullness in my life. I want to be empowered in order to live for You and experience You in a new way. I believe you desire this for me, more than I want it for myself. Baptise me now heavenly Father - so that I can never be the same.

Trusting You to answer me, I speak those things that are not as though they already were and confess that I am now Spirit-filled. I allow the rivers of living water to flow up out of my belly, as I yield my vocal chords and expect to speak in tongues as Your Spirit gives me utterance. I worship You over and over for this, in Jesus mighty name. Amen.

Keep Praying

As you keep praying the prayer above, (by incorporating your own words), I encourage you to keep praying and keep trusting God *until* you receive. Don't be discouraged. You need the fullness of the Spirit in your life. It's God's best for you.

"The coming of the Holy Spirit is dependent upon prayer... Even Christ was subject to this law of prayer. With him, it is, it ever has been, and ever will be, 'Ask, and it will be given you; seek and ye shall find; knock, and it shall be opened unto you…'

How complex, confusing, and involved is many a human direction about obtaining the gift of the Holy Spirit as… the one who empowers us. How simple and direct is our Lord's direction – ASK! This is plain and direct… Ask, seek, knock, till he comes… the Father's greatest gift and the child's greatest need, the Holy Spirit'" (Bounds 281, 283).

Until we Experience Change

"We need to go before God and stay there until we feel Him and are changed" (Johnson, Beni 104).

When you receive the fullness of the Spirit, you become enlightened; you change. You start thinking differently, talking and acting differently. You become liberated:

> By "the Lord" what I mean is the Spirit, and **in any heart where the Spirit of the Lord is present, <u>there is liberty</u>.**
>
> *(2 Corinthians 3:17 VOICE)*

"I became such a changed person that my natural instincts and reactions were replaced by the leading of the Spirit… 'For as many as are led by the Spirit of God, these are sons of God' (Romans 8:14)" (Hinn 65).

> *For if your life is just about satisfying the impulses of your sinful nature, then prepare to die. But if you have invited the Spirit to destroy these selfish desires, **you will***

experience life. If the Spirit of God is leading you,
then take comfort in knowing you are His children.
(Romans 8:13-14 VOICE)

So don't you see that we don't owe this old do-it-yourself
life one red cent. There's nothing in it for us, nothing
at all. **The best thing to do is give it a decent burial**
and get on with your new life. God's Spirit beckons.
There are things to do and places to go!
(Romans 8:13-14 MSG)

The limitations of our flesh start melting into the background, as we relinquish centre stage to God's Spirit.

Intense Peace and Joy!

The kingdom of God is not about eating and drinking.
When God reigns, the order of the day is redeeming justice,
true peace, and joy made possible by the Holy Spirit.
(Romans 14:17 VOICE)

There's joy unspeakable. In the presence of God is the fullness of joy. There is no *fullness* without Him.

The nearest I can describe the experience of God's presence on your life for the first time is, "ecstasy," intense and overwhelming joy!

If you have sincerely prayed and experienced real change today, then this is the first day of the rest of your life. Nothing will ever be the same.

Enjoy the fullness!

Dr Alan Pateman

CHAPTER 1

Tongues for Edification

If you lack Power charge the Battery

In his mini-book called, "Why Tongues" Kenneth E. Hagin wrote the following:

"In writing to the church at Corinth, Paul encouraged them to **continue the practice of speaking with other tongues in their worship of God and in their prayer lives** as a means of spiritual edification. Greek language scholars tell us that we have a word in our modern vernacular, which is closer to the meaning of the original than the word 'edified.'

That word is **'charge'** – as used in connection with charging a battery. Therefore we could paraphrase this verse, **'He that speaketh in an unknown tongue edifies, charges,**

builds himself up like a battery.' And this wonderful, supernatural means of spiritual edification – notice that it is not mental nor physical edification – is for every one of God's children" (Hagin, Why Tongues 13).

In his famous best selling book, "Prayer: Key to Revival" Dr Paul Cho wrote:

"Praying in your prayer language is the means by which you can build yourself up spiritually. I find that my prayer language is a great spiritual blessing to me. If we could not benefit from praying in the Holy Spirit, God would have never given this precious gift to us. Jesus Christ said before He ascended into heaven: **'And these signs shall follow them that believe; in my name shall they cast out devils; they shall speak with new tongues'** (Mark 16:17 KJV).

As a young Christian, I could not see the importance of tongues in my Christian life. **However, the longer I believe in Jesus Christ, the more I feel the tremendous importance of tongues in my own personal Christian life. I spend a good deal of my prayer life praying in my spiritual language.**

Like Paul, I pray in the Spirit, and I pray with my understanding also. In public, I would rather pray in a language which all can understand. Yet, in my personal prayer time, **I use my spiritual prayer language a great deal...**

Weaknesses or Power

The way to be strengthened, to help our infirmities (weaknesses), is praying in our prayer language. The Holy Spirit knows our spiritual need better than we do. However,

He will use our tongue to pray for our need. Praise the Lord for the Holy Spirit!" (Cho 126, 127,128)

And in his book, "The Code of the Holy Spirit" Perry Stone adds to this by saying, "The word *edify* refers to *building a house* which means that a person praying in the Spirit is *building his or her spiritual house*… **The house we are building is our inner spirit**, as each of our bodies is the temple of the Holy Spirit (1 Corinthians 3:16)" (Stone 50).

"When you pray in tongues your spirit prays… **your inner man is edified, strengthened, made sensitive and purified…** When you pray in tongues, you are talking to God. It is a wonderful way of communicating with Him and of exalting and praising Him… Your inner man is conveying your love and appreciation to God from deep inside" (Ekman, A Life of Victory 29).

Here are ten reasons believers should speak in tongues (with emphasis on private not public prayer):

1. Tongues the initial sign *(Acts 2:4)*

2. Tongues for spiritual edification *(1 Corinthians 14:4)*

3. Tongues remind us of the Spirit's indwelling presence *(John 14:16-17)*

4. Praying in tongues is praying in line with God's perfect will *(Romans 8:26-27)*

5. Praying in tongues stimulates faith *(Jude 20)*

6. Speaking in tongues, a means of keeping free from worldly contamination *(1 Corinthians 14:28)*

7. Praying in tongues enables us to pray for the unknown.

8. Praying in tongues gives spiritual refreshing *(Isaiah 28:11-12)*

9. Tongues for giving thanks *(1 Corinthians 14:15-17)*

10. Speaking in tongues brings the tongue under subjection *(James 3:8)*

This very clearly teaches us that praying in the Spirit helps build up our faith and spiritual muscles. We can even imagine that going to God, speaking in tongues and reading the Word is like going to a spiritual gym and building up our strength!

> *Build yourselves up [founded] on your most holy faith [make progress, rise like an edifice higher and higher], praying in the Holy Spirit.*
>
> *(Jude 20 AMP)*

According to Dr Paul Cho, "The word used for *building* in the original Greek language is **OIKODOMEW**, or *placing one block on another*. As in erecting a building, you can sense your faith actually being *built* as you pray in the Holy Spirit."

Faith level Built

Dr Cho went on to say, "Knowing that it is important for my messages to build faith and hope in the hearts of thousands of people, **I spend a good deal of time building my *own* faith level up by praying in the Holy Spirit...**

There is an internal struggle going on in the life of every Christian. The spirit is constantly warring against the flesh. By building yourself spiritually, you will find strength to overcome the flesh, which is trying to drag you down... To be a successful intercessor, you should... be willing to pray in the Holy Spirit" (Cho 127,128,130).

Tongues an Untapped Power House

Even if things look rosy now, we must *continually* build ourselves up, in preparation for what's up ahead. We never know what's coming down the pipe, so we must be ready for anything. To do this we must continually be going to God, drinking and soaking up His Spirit, so that rivers of living water continually flow to and through us *(for the benefit of others)*.

> *Now on the final and most important day of the Feast, Jesus stood, and He cried in a loud voice, **if any man is thirsty, let him come to Me and <u>drink</u>**! He who believes in Me [who cleaves to and trusts in and relies on Me] as the Scripture has said, **from his innermost being shall flow [continuously] springs and <u>rivers of living water</u>... he was speaking here of the Spirit...***
> *(John 7:37-39 AMP)*

According to the Strong's Concordance, the Greek word used for *rivers* is *potamos*, which has three definitions: *1. a stream (a river); 2. a torrent 3. floods (see G4215).*

Most Christians receive just a *drip-of-water* but God has promised us **torrents-of-life-giving-water.** It might help us to see tongues like a small generator inside of us that helps prime the pump in our spirits! The more we *"pump"* (*pray in tongues*) the more *"living water"* will flow! As a result we should see more of the Spirit moving in and through our lives.

"Speaking in tongues is the doorway to the other gifts of the Spirit. When it is opened, like **a floodgate, rivers of living water begin to flow, and other currents start to flow** with it. Rivers of healing, supernatural wisdom and supernatural power, also emerge" (Ekman, A Life of Victory 29).

Continuity is a big key in Prayer

"Pray without ceasing" (1 Thessalonians 5:17 KJV).

We must get in the flow and *stay* there. However praying in tongues should never be done out of emotion or nervous energy – but *by faith!* In other words it is NOT a religious-ritual or mantra. Romans 1:17 says, "The righteous shall live *by faith,"* this includes praying *by faith.* Everything in a believer's life must be legitimate and *"... by faith."*

> *His anointing teaches you about all things and as **that anointing is real, not counterfeit** - just as it has taught you, remain in him.*
>
> *(1 John 2:27)*

The anointing abides within us: "The anointing (the sacred appointment, the unction) which you received from Him abides [permanently] in you" *(1 John 2:27 AMP).* And it's praying in tongues that helps us stay focused and sensitive to this anointing within. We must ever be mindful of the supernatural. We are not just *carnal-earthlings!* Tongues help us with this; from beginning to end they are *supernatural!* So we must spend time priming our inner-pump. The heart of man is like deep water and to draw it out, it helps to pray in tongues.

> *Counsel in the heart of man is like water in a deep well,*
> *but **a man of understanding draws it out.***
> *(Proverbs 20:5 AMP)*

Every born-again, Spirit filled believer needs to yield to speaking in tongues, as it is one of the many effective ways that we can *increase* our sensitivity to the Spirit.

Tongues can bring Dramatic Results

For instance we should not wait for the anointing to *fall before we begin* praying in tongues. It's not an emotional endeavour that rests on feelings. Nor is there any need to *simulate* any special atmosphere. We prime the pump by faith. Each believer already possesses the anointing deep within; building ourselves up inwardly by using our prayer language, should be a daily discipline.

"There are many reasons given in the New Testament for believers speaking in tongues, or as I like to say, ***praying in the prayer language of the Spirit***" (Stone 50).

Paul was an advocate for *praying in the prayer language of the Spirit.* Stone continues, "Paul received the Holy Spirit when Ananias laid his hands upon him, and later Paul wrote he also spoke with tongues" (1 Corinthians 14:18).

> *It is written in the Law, By **men of strange languages***
> *and by the lips of foreigners will I speak to this people, and*
> *not even then will they listen to Me, says the Lord.*
> *(1 Corinthians 14:21 AMP)*

Paul, in this scripture was referring to Isaiah 28:11, *"No, but [the Lord will teach the rebels in a more humiliating way] by men with stammering lips and another tongue will He speak to this people [says Isaiah, and teach them His lessons]" (Isaiah 28:11 AMP).* This was a prophecy given by the prophet Isaiah, telling the people of Israel, that God was going to use other people, not just the Jews, to speak to the Jewish nation.

*When they heard this sound, a crowd came together in bewilderment, because each one heard them speaking in his own language. Utterly amazed, they asked: "Are not all these men who are speaking Galileans? Then **how is it that each of us hears them in his own native language?"***

(Acts 2:6-8)

On the day of Pentecost when the one hundred and twenty disciples were altogether, as they began to speak in tongues, it caused a great commotion to the people listening.

*While Peter was still speaking these words, **the Holy Spirit came on all who heard the message.** The circumcised believers who had come with Peter were astonished that the gift of **the Holy Spirit had been poured out even on the Gentiles.** For they heard them speaking in tongues and praising God.*

(Acts 10:44-46)

Tongues as a Sign to the Unbeliever

Tongues are for a sign, not to the believing, but to the unbelieving.

(1 Corinthians 14:22)

We may think that we are just speaking in tongues, but there are times when someone may understand what is being said.

There have been many reported instances of this. For instance, during the Gulf war, there was a young man, serving in the forces, who was born-again. He was on guard duty at an air base, and not having had time to spend with the Lord, he started to pray out in tongues. Afterwards some Muslim pilots approached him wanting to know more about this Jesus he had been talking about.

It seems that by praying out loud in tongues, he had been actually speaking about Jesus in their own language. The result was that they all gave their lives to the Lord!

Heart Secrets Revealed

In like manner, Perry Stone writes: "Another purpose for speaking in tongues is that when the Spirit manifests in a setting with *unbelievers*, **the Spirit can reveal the secrets of men's hearts and become a** *sign to the unbeliever* **of the reality of God and His power.**

I have personally witnessed this manifestation on several occasions, as at times the Holy Spirit would speak through a believer in tongues and a person from a foreign nation would understand each word spoken by the believer who was speaking in tongues."

Perry goes on to describe: "I recall years ago during an Israel tour that our group was in the Kidron Valley in Jerusalem. A small group of Arab teens were about fifty yards away, and I could see a mischievous look on their faces. I saw one pick up a rock, and I know he intended to throw it. I looked at two men and said, 'Follow me.' I approached the boys and began speaking in other tongues through the Holy Spirit. I was speaking a language they all understood.

The leader looked at me, laid down the rock, and walked away. After this, the men said, 'What were you saying to them?' The Lord gave me the interpretation. I told them that I said, 'The Lord is revealing to me that you boys are planning on throwing rocks at my group. He is telling me that your hearts are unclean, as dirty as the filth and garbage you see in this valley. These are God's people, and if you harm any one of them, God is going to severely punish you, so leave now.' This was an operation of the Spirit. **The secrets of their hearts were exposed"** (Stone 51, 53).

> ...*as the secrets of their hearts are laid bare. So they will fall down and worship God, exclaiming, "God is really among you!"*
>
> *(1 Corinthians 14:25)*

God is God and He knows what is needed at any specific moment of time. (He even knows the local vernacular of any culture!) So if we are sensitive and obedient to His Spirit, we too can be used in this way, we just need to make ourselves available.

❖

CHAPTER 2

Tongues for Worship

I n the last chapter the many uses of tongues has already been discussed; we as believers, can communicate directly with God in tongues. Now let's discuss briefly how tongues also play an important role in our worship, (both privately and in public meetings).

> *So what shall I do?* ***I will pray with my spirit,*** *but I will also pray with my understanding;* ***I will <u>sing</u> with my spirit,*** *but I will also sing with my understanding.*
> *(1 Corinthians 14:15)*

In his book called, "Good Morning Holy Spirit" Benny Hinn describes the impact that the Holy Spirit had on his prayer life, including the fact that he began *singing spiritual songs* and didn't know why!

"Three things happened when the Holy Spirit entered my life.

- **First** the Word of the Living God became absolute life to me...

- **Second,** my prayer life changed completely. Gone were the hours of praying, yawning, and repeating myself. The Holy Spirit and I were in conversation. He made God real. He gave me power and a boldness that made me feel ten feet tall.

- **Third,** He transformed my daily Christian life. **I actually began to sing** and didn't know why until I read the words:

'Be filled with the Spirit, speaking to one another in psalms and hymns and **spiritual songs, singing and making melody in your heart to the Lord'** (Ephesians 5:18-19 NKJV)" (Hinn 64-65).

Heavenly Vocabulary

When we are worshipping God, it is only natural for us to keep reverting to our heavenly language - "tongues." Sometimes when we come before the Lord worshipping and praising Him, we do not have the vocabulary to express or articulate the depth of our love and adoration for Him (as our intellects are limited). This is when the eloquence of our spirit man must take over and start singing expressively, spontaneously and freely in tongues!

Holy Intimacy

We can compare it to the married man, who is with his wife. He alone has that right to be intimate with her. Married couples have their own way of talking to each other, *a secret language!* Likewise we too have an intimate relationship with the Father *(but non-romantic of course!)* and when we start worshipping Him – by entering into His presence - it is only natural for us to start speaking in that *intimate way.*

"When I began this journey… I fell madly in love with the Holy Spirit. I touched a realm that I had never experienced before. I am now so very addicted to His presence; His realm is where I always want to dwell" (Johnson, Beni 102).

It's impossible to worship without love, which can also be explained this way: it's impossible to worship from a place of disobedience! Jesus repeatedly revealed this love/ obedience connection in the fourteenth chapter of the book of John. **Worship has everything to do with love - love has everything to do with obedience:**

> *If you love me, keep my commands... Whoever has my commands and keeps them is the one who loves me...*
>
> *Anyone who loves me will obey my teaching... Anyone who does not love me will not obey my teaching...*
>
> *(John 14:15-24)*

Hollow-Habits & Learned-Behaviour

True worship can only come out of pure love. The only way that God knows if we love Him or not, is if we obey Him or not. Singing songs and offering mere lip service reveals nothing of the heart: "These people honour me with their lips, but their hearts are far from me" (Matthew 15:8).

I prefer how the Message bible puts this particular verse: "Frauds! Isaiah's prophecy of you hit the bull's-eye: These people make a big show of saying the right thing, but their heart isn't in it. **They act like they're worshiping me, but they don't mean it. They just use me...**" (MSG)

Perhaps even more telling are the following accounts of Isaiah's prophecy, taken directly from the Old Testament:

*Forasmuch as this people draw near Me with their mouth and honour Me with their lips but remove their hearts and minds far from Me, and **their fear and reverence for Me are a commandment of men that is learned by repetition without any thought as to the meaning**...*
(AMP)

*Their worship of Me consists of **man-made traditions learned** by rote; it is a meaningless sham...*
(Isaiah 29:13 VOICE)

The Amplified bible's account perfectly describes *learned-behaviour*: "**...learned by repetition without any thought as to the meaning,**" our worship must be much more than just another heartless ritual.

We were all subject to some form of conditioning right from birth! But the point is this: worship is a condition of the heart. It's not about what we *do*, as much as what we *are!* (True or false worshippers John 4:23-24).

The good thing about using tongues during worship, is that we can't easily make a ritual out of them. For instance we can't memorise or learn them. We can't predict, control or manipulate them either! While copies and counterfeits exist, *authentic* **tongues cannot be a learned behaviour!** Matter of fact, they are one of the few things in life that are genuinely pure and must be regarded as such (Romans 14:16).

Liquid Heaven

Unrestricted tongues used during true worship are rich and fluid; like the wind nothing can contain or control them (in a wrong way). My wife likes to describe this true worship experience as **"liquid heaven!"** because heaven pours out on those who worship God from a pure heart.

God seeks true worship from true worshippers. I enjoy the sheer visual element of this passage below; that my heavenly Father is seeking me out! My heartfelt genuine worship is prized by Him; treasured and cherished. As a genuine worshipper, I am valuable to Him:

> *The hour cometh, and now is, when the **true worshippers shall worship the Father in spirit and in truth: for the Father seeketh such to worship him.** God is a Spirit: and they that worship him must worship him in spirit and in truth.*
>
> *(John 4:23-24 KJV)*

The scripture above gives the impression of a thorough investigation! But what exactly is God seeking for in a true worshipper? At this point we must remember what

2 Chronicles 16:9 revealed: IT HAS ALWAYS BEEN ABOUT THE HEART!

> **For the eyes of the Lord run to and fro throughout the whole earth,** *to shew himself strong in the behalf of them whose* **HEART** **is perfect toward him.**
> *(2 Chronicles 16:9 KJV)*

Heart of a Worshipper

"King David towers above all other Old Testament figures in this sense — he is remembered not so much for the greatness of his actions, but for the greatness of his heart for God. **His passionate heart set him apart in God's eyes long before he ever won great military victories...**

While David was still in obscurity, God saw that he was a man after His own heart (see Acts 13:22). What was the evidence of David's heart after God? Scripture indicates two primary aspects of David's life before he was anointed king.

First, when nobody was looking, when nobody was calling prayer meetings or leading a revival in Judah, **David was pouring out his heart in worship and prayer to God** in the fields where he tended his father's sheep.

With no one around, his pursuit of God was motivated by nothing but a desire to know God for His own sake.

David's relationship with the Lord was highly unusual for his day because the entire paradigm for worship in Israel at the time was focused on the sacrifice of animals to temporarily deal with sin, and not the sacrifice of praise from the heart.

His heart led him beyond the letter of the law to the heart of the Lord, Himself.

Secondly, David's battles against the lion and the bear **revealed his heart for God because he relied completely on God for victory.** This trust indicated that David's heart for the Lord was not something that changed according to his circumstances. He had integrity of heart. (See 1 Samuel 17:37)" (Johnson, Bill, Strengthen Yourself in The Lord 11-12).

In Worship the Heart must Rule

In worship we must allow our hearts and not our heads to rule. Our minds will tell us not to sing out in tongues but we must *step-out* **regardless, in pure adoration and worship.**

Amusingly have you ever tried thinking in tongues! [It doesn't work – try it!] Our prayer language simply bypasses our minds and comes directly from our spirit man. Thus making it pure – without need for filtering - and is so very valuable in God's economy!

"Speaking in tongues as a prayer language is a pure form of communication – spirit to Spirit – or your spirit speaking to God" (Stone 50).

"…no man can understand your prayer language except God, **your prayer cannot be hindered by opposing spiritual forces, as Daniel experienced.** Your spirit can communicate unhindered directly with the Father through the Holy Spirit" (Cho 127).

So tongues are a **"pure form of communication,"** that our overly analytical minds can't meddle with!

Thankfully then tongues can bypass any rational or intellectual interference. They simply don't require our sophisticated mental approval to work!

"Your mind does not get in the way or limit your prayers, because you are praying directly from your spirit. The Holy Spirit can then lead you to pray in tongues in many ways, rather than just one way. There is tremendous variation in the Spirit to meet the many different needs and situations that confront mankind" (Ekman, A Life of Victory 29).

In fact we tend to miss-trust what we can't control and for this reason tongues remain underestimated and still lack priority for many in the Body of Christ today.

Customarily we micro-manage all the drama and incidentals but side step the major and more significant issues of life. **Tongues have the power to make an *atomic* difference in our lives and yet an air of *indifference* about it persists.**

Not Drunk as You Suppose!

We tend to have a spirit of miss-trust towards whatever we don't understand. As a result we make random assumptions and reduce everything down to our own level of thinking.

During Pentecost these international onlookers (from all over the world) responded in much the same way. They heard the believers speaking "the wonderful works of God" in their own languages (which was an impossibility) and were initially "amazed." But in rapid succession they go from **"amazement,"** and **"doubting,"** to **"mocking!"** A process we all go through when we fail to understand something properly. [In fact it's a psychological hard wiring in people, to *discredit* whatever threatens them or can't be explained].

> *The multitude came together, and were **confounded,** because that **every man heard them speak in his own language.** And they were all amazed and marveled…*
>
> *…we do hear them speak in our tongues <u>the wonderful works of God</u>.*
>
> *And they were all **amazed**, and were in **doubt**, saying one to another, What meaneth this? Others **mocking** said, these men are full of new wine.*
> (Acts 2:4-8, 11-13 KJV)

So we must not allow ourselves to be limited and as Ephesians 6:18 tells us, we must *"Pray in the Spirit on all occasions…"* and this would include worship! *"…we do hear them speak in our tongues <u>the wonderful works of God</u>."*

Prayer and worship go hand in hand. Tongues must not be stifled, underestimated or quenched. In fact during worship, tongues should be *intensified!*

Worship and Power

Finally in his book "Breaking the Power of Evil," Rick Joyner writes about the influence - that was **John Wimber!** Whose extraordinary legacy, was one of worship and power:

"In my opinion, one of the greatest Christian movements during the 1980s and '90s was the Vineyard Movement led by John Wimber. Though I was never officially a member of this movement, I did get to know John Wimber quite well, and I ministered in some of his conferences and churches.

I marveled many times at the extraordinary authority that John, his leaders, and so many people in Vineyard churches had over demons. I witnessed some of the strongest evil spirits I had ever seen come out of people with a word - from an usher!

Yet, almost no one thought of the Vineyard as a major deliverance ministry. **Rather, they were best known for their worship and for healing. That is the way it should be.**

True Worship comes from Seeing the Lord

True worship does not come in order to see the Lord; it comes from seeing the Lord. If we see Him, we will worship! To the degree that we see Him with the eyes of our hearts, we will worship.

We need many times as much worship in our life as warfare. We have too many examples of people who become overly focused on fighting demons who have taken on the nature of the demons they are casting out of people.

Those who spend too much time studying cults often start to take on a more foul spirit than the cults they study. That is because of the spiritual principle highlighted in Second Corinthians 3:18, which states that we will **become what we are beholding…**

We are here to fight battles on the earth, but let us always heed the exhortation of Colossians 3:1-2 (NASB):

*Therefore if you have been raised up with Christ, **keep seeking the things above, where Christ is,** seated at the right hand of God. **Set your mind on the things above, not on the things that are on earth.***

The primary way that we will win our battles on the earth is by dwelling in the heavenly places with Christ and bringing evidence of Heaven - the Kingdom of God - to the earth" (Joyner, Breaking the Power of Evil 22-23).

❖

CHAPTER 3

Tongues for Intercession

Called by name Zechariah refers to the Holy Spirit as the Spirit of Prayer. *"I'll pour a spirit of grace and prayer over them.* They'll then be able to recognize me…" *(Zechariah 12:10 MSG)*

Many of us started out the same way that Beni Johnson did, "I prayed because I thought that was what I was supposed to do. I did not pray out of relationship with the Holy Spirit" (Johnson, Beni 22). We must all become more conscious of the Holy Spirit in our daily lives, but especially in prayer.

"How are you led by the Spirit? You become familiar with His voice. You recognise it. You respond to it. And the more you fellowship with Him, the deeper the relationship becomes" (Hinn 65).

Our Helper and Prayer Guide

Once we know the Holy Spirit our prayer lives become revolutionised.

"**The Holy Spirit's guidance is the most valuable asset we have for prayer.** The Holy Spirit knows the Father's heart and will (1 Corinthians 2:10-12). He takes what is in the Father's heart and puts it in our hearts and **helps us to pray it through...** Sometimes we do not know how we should pray, but God's Spirit knows. Therefore, the scriptures beseech us to pray in the spirit – pray in other tongues (1 Corinthians 14:15).

Praying in other tongues is an invaluable resource, which transcends the limitations of the intellect. God's Spirit can take what is in the Father's heart and bring it to fruition through the prayer of the believer **who prays in the Spirit.**

Everything that God has given us in our church, bible school and missionary work, has come through this type of prayer" (Ekman, The Church of the Living God 67-68).

"The Christian if left to himself does not know how to pray nor how he ought to pray. But God has stooped to meet us in this helplessness of ours by giving us the Holy Spirit himself to pray for us. **That operation of His Spirit is deeper than our thought or feeling, but is acknowledged and answered by God.**

Our first work, therefore, ought to be to come into God's presence not with our ignorant prayers, not with many words and thoughts, but in the **confidence that the Divine work of the Holy Spirit is being carried on within us**" (Murray 55).

The Interceding Holy Spirit

When we start interceding in tongues, the Holy Spirit is not *idly* sitting by listening; rather He starts to intercede on our behalf.

> *In the same way, the Spirit helps us in our weakness. We do not know what we ought to pray for, but **the Spirit himself intercedes for us with groans** that words cannot express.*
>
> *(Romans 8:26)*

"We pray not by the truth the Holy Spirit reveals to us, but we pray by the actual presence of the Holy Spirit. He puts the desire in our hearts; kindles that desire by his own flame. We simply give lip and voice and heart to his unutterable groanings.

Our prayers are taken up by him and energized and sanctified by his intercession... He prays for us, through us and in us... He puts the prayer in us and we give it utterance and heart" (Bounds 289).

Following His Lead

In Romans 8:26 above it said, "...but the Spirit himself intercedes for us with **groans** that words cannot express." Just as the Holy Spirit groans with strange noises, we too can do the same. When we start interceding for someone, we use our own language, but we also need to use our heavenly language. When we start interceding using tongues, it helps take what we are interceding for, out of this earth realm and into the realm of the spirit.

Praying in the Spirit helps us overcome our weaknesses and uncertainty about what to pray for. It's usually because of ignorance or insensitivity that we go through any day not hearing from the voice of God.

However when we do feel moved about a certain situation or person, yet don't understand or know what's really happening, then we must pray in tongues - giving the situation over to God – this way we are being faithful and obedient with the unction to pray and not just dull, hard of hearing or stubborn.

According to His Will

To pray the will of God, we must pray in tongues; inspired tongues are always according to His will.

> *He who searches our hearts knows the mind of the Spirit, because* **the Spirit intercedes for the saints in accordance with God's will.**
>
> *(Romans 8:27)*

> **This is the confidence** *(the assurance, the privilege of boldness) which we have in Him: [we are sure] that* **if we ask anything (make any request) according to His will (in agreement with His own plan), He listens to and hears us.**

And if (since) we [positively] know that He listens to us in whatever we ask, we also know [with settled and absolute knowledge] **that we have [granted us as our present possessions] the requests made of Him.**

(1 John 5:14 AMP)

According to E.M Bounds, **"We always pray according to the will of God when the Holy Spirit helps our praying.** He prays through us only 'according to the will of God.' If our prayers are not according to the will of God they die in the presence of the Holy Spirit. He gives such prayers no countenance, no help" (Bounds 289).

So praying in the Spirit affords us great confidence. In her book "The Happy Intercessor" Beni Johnson talks about tongues as part of intercession routine and her dependence on the Holy Spirit.

She writes, "What about praying in the Spirit; how does praying in tongues become intercession? For an intercessor, tongues play an important role as we pray. I spend a lot of time praying in tongues.

I like to use my prayer language when I take walks. As I walk, I begin praying in tongues, and I can feel my spirit begin to engage with the Holy Spirit. **As I continue to pray, things will come to my mind, and I will speak in tongues over those things...** engaging with our spirit language causes our prayers to become effective" (Johnson, Beni 235).

Enabling Agent in God's Dispensation of Doing

It's only as we engage with the Holy Spirit that our great commission can be fulfilled:

"The Holy Spirit is not only the bright lamp of the Christian dispensation, its teacher and guide, but is the divine helper. **He is the enabling agent in God's new dispensation of doing.** As the pilot takes his stand at the wheel to guide the vessel, so the Holy Spirit takes up abode in the heart to guide and empower all its efforts.

The Holy Spirit executes the whole gospel through the man by his presence and control of the spirit of man... the Holy Spirit is the one efficient agent, absolute and indispensable.

The gospel cannot be executed *but by the Holy Spirit.* He only has the regal authority to do this royal work. **Intellect cannot execute it, neither can learning, nor eloquence, nor truth, not even the revealed truth can execute the gospel...**

Not any, nor all of these, though spoken with angelic wisdom, angelic eloquence, can execute the gospel with saving power. **Only tongues set on fire by the Holy Spirit can witness the saving power of Christ with power to save others"** (Bounds 280).

❖

CHAPTER 4

Diversities of Levels

Jack W. Hayford says, "'*Praying with all prayer and supplication in the spirit,*' must be - indeed cannot be otherwise - recognised as referring to spiritual language, for essentially the same terminology is utilised in 1 Corinthians 14:14-16. We read, '*For if I pray in a tongue, my spirit prays... So... I will pray with my spirit.*'

We cannot tell whether the word '*spirit*' should be capitalised or not in either passage. But whether it refers to my spirit or the Holy Spirit, '*praying with the spirit,*' involves speaking in tongues" (Hayford 133).

Ephesians 6:18 says:

> *And pray in the Spirit on all occasions with all kinds of prayers and requests. With this in mind, be alert and always keep on praying for all the saints.*

This is to be used at all times with all perseverance for all the saints and is to be *"in the spirit."* Without pressing the point too hard, this is probably *"praying in tongues"* it certainly includes it.

So, there is praying with the mind and praying with the spirit *(1 Corinthians 14:5)*. Paul knew the blessing of this unlearned language of the Spirit. While giving instruction on its use in the Church, he said, *"I thank God that I speak in tongues more than all of you" (1 Corinthians 14:18).*

Experiencing direct Communication

I believe Paul communicated with God continually by speaking in tongues. **He was aware that in so doing, his own spirit was experiencing direct communication with the Lord, and was *edifying* himself in the process** *(1 Corinthians 14:4 also Jude 20).*

> *Now about spiritual gifts, brothers, I do not want you to be ignorant.*
> *(1 Corinthians 12:1)*

Intercession can be done in our own understanding using our earthly language, or we can pray in the Spirit in tongues.

> *Now there are **distinctive varieties** and distributions of endowments (gifts, extraordinary powers distinguishing certain Christians, due to the power of divine grace operating in their souls by the Holy Spirit) and they vary, but the [Holy] Spirit remains the same.*

And there are distinctive varieties of service and ministration, but it is the same Lord [Who is served]. And there are distinctive varieties of operation [of working to accomplish things], but it is the same God Who inspires and energizes them all in all.

(1 Corinthians 12:4-5 AMP)

Then what am I to do? **I will pray with my spirit [by the Holy Spirit that is within me], but I will also pray [intelligently] with my mind and understanding;** *I will sing with my spirit [by the Holy Spirit that is within me], but I will sing* **[intelligently] with my mind and understanding also.**

(1 Corinthians 14:15 AMP)

*When the day of Pentecost came and they were all in one place. Suddenly a sound like the blowing of a **violent wind** came from heaven and filled the whole house where they were sitting. They saw what seemed to be tongues of fire that separated and came to rest on each of them. All of them were filled with the Holy Spirit and began to **speak in other tongues as the Spirit enabled them.***

(Acts 2:1-4)

When they heard this sound, a crowd came together in bewilderment, because each one heard them speaking in his own language. Utterly amazed, they asked: "Are not all these men who are speaking Galileans? Then how is it that each of us hears them in his own native language?"

(Acts 2:6-8)

As believers, who are Spirit filled, it is important to have an understanding of our prayer language. God gave tongues to us, through the power of the Holy Spirit. We must know how to use our tongues in the right way.

...and I have filled him with the Spirit of God, with skill, ability and knowledge in all kinds of crafts.

(Exodus 31:3)

Don't be Ignorant

God does not want us to remain in ignorance. He has given us His Holy Spirit, wisdom and a full understanding in every area of our lives, including tongues. On the other hand, Satan will try and keep us ignorant, to stop us from developing our heavenly tongue, and learning that in tongues we have a powerful tool.

In Ephesians 1:18, Paul says: *"I pray also that the eyes of your heart may be enlightened in order that you may know the hope to which he has called you."*

In 1 Corinthians 14:2, Paul tells us:

For anyone who speaks in a tongue does not speak to men but to God. Indeed, no-one understands him; **he utters mysteries <u>with his spirit</u>.**

(1 Corinthians 14:2)

For one who speaks in an [unknown] tongue speaks not to men but **to God,** *for no one understands or catches his meaning, because in the [Holy] Spirit he utters secret truths and hidden things [not obvious to the understanding].*

(1 Corinthians 14:2 AMP)

There are different kinds of gifts, but the same Spirit. There are different kinds of service, but the same Lord. There are different kinds of working, but the same God works all of them in all men. Now to each one the manifestation of the Spirit is given for the common good.

(1 Corinthians 12:4-7)

The disciples and those early believers first received the Holy Spirit on the day of Pentecost.

*When the day of Pentecost came, they were all together in one place. Suddenly a sound like the blowing of a violent wind came from heaven and **filled the <u>whole</u> house** where they were sitting. They saw what seemed to be tongues of fire that separated and came to rest **on <u>each</u> of them. <u>All</u> of them were filled** with the Holy Spirit and **began to speak in other tongues <u>as the Spirit enabled them</u>.***

(Acts 2:1-4)

A Sign of Baptism

Tongues is a sign that we are filled with the Holy Spirit, a heavenly language that can only be received after having received the baptism of the Holy Spirit. People must be open to receiving the Holy Spirit; tongues are the manifestation, the outward sign that they have received Him.

While Peter was still speaking these words, the Holy Spirit came on all who heard the message. The circumcised believers who had come with Peter were astonished that the gift of the Holy Spirit had been poured out even on the

*Gentiles. For they heard them **speaking in tongues and praising God.***

(Acts 10:44-46)

*And these signs will accompany those who believe: In my name they will drive out demons; **they will speak in new tongues.***

(Mark 16:17)

Speaking in tongues is a *supernatural* utterance, given by the Holy Spirit, in a language never learned by the person. It brings us into the realm of the *supernatural*; it makes the *supernatural* more tangible to us.

We live in an earthly kingdom and speak our earthly language. The Kingdom of God also has its own language. When we become born-again and receive the baptism of the Holy Spirit, we also receive tongues, our heavenly language.

Tongues, then, are a sign, not for believers but for unbelievers...

(1 Corinthians 14:22)

A lot of people complain that we pray in tongues too much, but Paul writes in 1 Corinthians 12:30 *"Do all speak in tongues?"* We know from experience that not all Christians do, although Paul spoke in tongues more than anyone else in the Corinthian church. 1 Corinthians 14:5 says, *"I would like every one of you to speak in tongues."*

Bringing us into the Fullness of the Spirit

God desires that all His people speak in tongues, and of course there *are no set rules for the length of time we have to spend praying in tongues.* Speaking and praying in tongues can bring us into the fullness of the Spirit. God has personality, **His language also has personality; it is not a *droning* (monotone) language without any life or expression in it. No! Heavenly language is expressive and full of life.**

When we pray or sing in tongues, they are not just *idle words,* every syllable has a meaning in the spirit realm. **We as born-again-Spirit-filled-believers have been given the privilege of entering into the supernatural realm: this is achieved by simply praying in tongues.**

We need to take full advantage of this privilege, for if we don't it would be like paying a lot of money to go on a mystery tour, and then sitting on the chair in the hotel room, refusing to go out!

Different Gifts but the same Spirit

The gift of *tongues* is for the Body of Christ to use personally in their private lives, but it is also for their use in public ministry (*individually and corporately*). Mark 16:17, states that signs will accompany those who *believe,* and it carries on to say *"they will drive out demons they will speak in new <u>tongues</u>"* (Mark 16:17).

When tongues are spoken out in public meetings it should *always* be followed by the interpretation, this will stop any confusion.

Paul wrote in his letter to the Corinthians, that when we get together, each of us should have a hymn, teaching or revelation to give to the Body. We are obviously being told to *speak out* in church.

In 1 Corinthians 14:27 he goes on to say:

If anyone speaks in a tongue, two - or at the most three - should speak, one at a time, and someone must interpret. If there is no interpreter, the speaker should keep quiet in the church and speak to himself and God.

(1 Corinthians 14:27)

He also wrote:

I would like every one of you to speak in tongues, but I would rather have you prophesy. He who prophesies is greater than one who speaks in tongues, unless he interprets, so that the church may be edified.

(1 Corinthians 14:5)

In chapter 12 it says:

*There are different kinds of gifts, but the same Spirit. There are different kinds of service, but the same Lord. There are different kinds of working, but the same God works all of them in all men... To another the ability to speak in **different kinds of tongues,** and to still another the **interpretation of tongues.***

(1 Corinthians 12:4-6,10)

Appreciate and Use Tongues

We must put away any fears or inhibitions, and start speaking out in tongues during our meetings. If we get the interpretation of our own tongue or someone else's, speak it out. **Satan will bombard us with doubt and fear,** he will tell us *"this is not the right time to speak out in tongues,"* or *"that interpretation cannot be from God, you are going to make a show of yourself."*

Satan is the accuser of the brethren and has always mocked tongues; it poses a real threat to him and so it's in his interest to subvert and undermine them.

"Do not let anyone despise such a unique spiritual gift. First Corinthians 14:39 tells us, 'Do not forbid speaking in tongues.' The devil, of course, does not like people to be baptized in the Spirit, nor does he like God's spiritual gifts.

He tries to stop the flow of God's power, wisdom and presence both within and around you. **Therefore, he often makes fun of tongues and ridicules it to hinder or limit its use.**

People can go to excesses in anything, but **do not let the fear of that hinder you from speaking a lot in tongues...** Do not let anyone hinder, limit or ridicule the gift God has given you. Learn how, when and why you are to use it, and **never neglect it.** First Timothy 4:14 states, 'Do not neglect your gift, which was given you' but 'fan into flame the gift of God, which is in you...' 2 Timothy 1:6" (Ekman, A Life of Victory 29-30).

Fear is a Non-negotiable!

So we can't afford to listen to the enemy's lies. Instead we must be confident, knowing that if we are right *before God and flowing in His Spirit,* then what comes out of us will be of Him. And with confidence we must be available and obedient to speak out in tongues (or give the interpretation), as God directs and gives the utterance.

God did not give us a spirit of timidity (of cowardice, of craven and cringing and fawning fear), but [He has given

us a spirit] of <u>power</u> and of <u>love</u> and of calm and <u>well-balanced mind</u> and discipline and self-control.
(2 Timothy 1:7 AMP)

In his book, "Keep Your Love On" Danny Silk discusses the power of love versus the weakness of fear, "Fear and love have opposite agendas and opposite strategies... They cannot coexist in a person, relationship, or culture.

God is very clear that the Spirit He put in you is not the spirit of fear, but the Spirit of love... **partnering with the Spirit of love is the way to displace fear in your life."**

*There is no fear in love [dread does not exist], but full-grown (complete, perfect) **love turns fear out of doors and expels every trace of terror!** For fear brings with it the thought of punishment, and [so] he who is afraid has not reached the full maturity of love [is not yet grown into love's complete perfection].*
(1 John 4:18 AMP)

"If you want to partner with the Holy Spirit, then you must have a strict 'no tolerance' policy about fear and punishment in your life...

Learning to partner with the Spirit of love requires you to become powerful ...the spirit of fear, is the spirit of powerlessness and a weak, divided mind.

When you grow up partnering with the spirit of fear, as most of us do, you learn to simply hand over your brain and your power, letting fear take control.

But as soon as you decide to partner with the Spirit of love, you have to think and make powerful choices" (Silk 93-94).

Born to be Fearless

As you continue reading the book that's in your hand, you will discover how to partner with God's Spirit and re-discover this powerful and supernatural prayer language that He has put at our disposal, so long as we operate from a right spirit.

Jesus expects us to know our true native origin, in other words, *"what sort of spirit"* we come from. He rebuked His disciples for their ignorance in this very area:

> *Lord, do You wish us to command fire to come down from heaven and consume them... He turned and rebuked and severely censured them...* **You do not know of what sort of spirit you are,** *for the Son of Man did not come to destroy men's lives, but to save them...*
> *(Luke 9:53-56 AMP)*

So what is the right spirit and how can we be sure to stay in that right spirit? The answer is LOVE. "For God so love the world..." We must - as Jesus demonstrated – love God and His people. God is love. God is Spirit and His influence on us is love.

"What began to happen to me was not natural - it was supernatural. The Spirit had taken over. **He began to baptise me with a love for people...** It was exactly as the

Word declared: **'the love of God has been poured out in our hearts by the Holy Spirit who was given us'** (Romans 5:5 NKJV)" (Hinn 65).

In no instance then can we afford to partner with a wrong spirit. The spirit of fear and love cannot co-exist. Our lives must be based on one or the other. As Danny Silk said above, our love for God and for His people must be our influence, to make us **"think and make powerful choices."**

It's self-evident. Only as we partner with the Spirit of love can we become a fearless and powerful influence on our generation!

❖

CHAPTER 5

God's Mouthpiece

God wants to talk and communicate with His people. He doesn't communicate by speaking out of the clouds or by using inanimate objects - He uses *us*. **We are His mouthpieces here on earth, so it is important that we are sensitive and obedient to His Holy Spirit.**

When we speak in tongues, there comes a moment when everyone is waiting for the interpretation. **When done properly, it's not just someone speaking their *own* thoughts; instead they are receiving something from the Holy Spirit.** It may be a thought, a vision or prophecy for the church, city or nation.

Someone could be speaking in tongues for just a couple of seconds but the interpretation could go on for a lot

longer. However we should not judge interpretation by its length, but by the spirit behind it. Paul says in 1 Corinthians 14:29 *"let two or three prophets speak, and let the other judge."*

When we speak in tongues our spirits are in communication with the Spirit of God. When we get an interpretation, it's not going to be in a different language (that no one understands) and *we do not take on different accents!* God uses our own voice for the interpretation.

Developing our Heavenly Language

*One who speaks in an [unknown] tongue speaks not to men but to God, for no one understands or catches his meaning, because in the [Holy] Spirit he **utters secret truths and hidden things** [not obvious to the understanding].*

(*1 Corinthians 14:2 AMP*)

*A person speaking in an unknown language is not addressing the church because he is really addressing God - those who overhear don't understand because he is **speaking in the Spirit the depths of the mysteries of the Lord.***

(*VOICE*)

Tongues is the communication tool, the key to the realm of the supernatural. It is direct communication between the Father and us. This has only been possible since the day of Pentecost. Before we were baptised in the Holy Spirit, there was no way of directly communicating with Him.

There are times when we are praising and worshipping God, and then run out of words to speak or sing. Our spirits then takeover and we start speaking or singing in tongues; it just flows like a river. This is when our spirits are in deep communication with the Holy Spirit. It is a time of drawing close to God and coming into His presence in the Holy of Holies.

> *If you praise him in the private language of tongues,* **God understands you but no one else does,** *for you are sharing intimacies just between you and him.*
> *(1 Corinthians 14:2 MSG)*

Receiving His Guidance

When He, the Spirit of Truth (the Truth-giving Spirit) comes, **He will guide you into all the Truth.**
(John 16:13 AMP)

Perry Stone writes, "Christ speaks to us through His written Word we call the New Testament. The Father speaks to us through the inward voice and divine guidance of His presence in our daily life, and **the Holy Spirit can and does speak to us using the prayer language** of the Holy Spirit, which is given to those who will believe and accept the gift. **Thus we have God's Word and illumination with us at all times, allowing the Spirit to <u>guide</u> us into all truth**" (Stone 54).

"Begin to pray… then stop and listen. You will get more understanding as you listen to the whisper of the Holy Spirit. He will tell you more. **As He tells you more, begin to pray what He is telling you.** In doing this, you are focused and you become targeted to the purpose of God. Your spirit and mind have become one with Heaven…" (Johnson, Beni 52)

Idols of Busyness and Self-reliance

Concerning the guidance of the Holy Spirit, I felt drawn to a passage in Isaiah the other day, in my personal study. And for this particular passage in Isaiah 30, the VOICE bible is a good choice of translation.

Isaiah is warning the people about their busyness and their lack of compliance to the leading of the Spirit: *"In returning and rest, you will be saved. In quietness and trust you will find strength. But you refused.* **You couldn't sit still...** *"* *(Isaiah 30:15-16 VOICE)*

Imagine! Just how relevant this is for us today! Our endless busyness and self-reliance do create a real conflict and interference, especially when it comes to being led of the Holy Spirit in our every day lives.

The Voice bible notes: "God invites His people to lean only on Him. If they will just stop their **busyness and self-reliance,** God will be able to take care of them."

We are our own worst enemy! And Isaiah stresses that only those **willing to be led** of God's Spirit, will experience true happiness in life. In verse 18 of the same chapter Isaiah goes on to say: *"Those inclined toward Him,* **waiting for His help,** *will find happiness..."*

And in verses 20-21 Isaiah distinctively describes the leading of the Holy Spirit by saying: *"...your great Teacher will reveal Himself to you; your eyes will see Him.* **Your ears will hear sweet words behind you: 'Go this way. There is your path; this is how you should go'** *whenever you must decide whether to turn to the right or the left..."*

How we all need this gentle guidance as described above! What a relief to know that we can have such assistance too. However in verses 22a and 23a Isaiah concludes by warning them, *"get rid of all your worthless idols …then God will see to it that your efforts are fruitful…"*

I would suggest at this point, that **busyness and self-reliance** most certainly become idols in our 21st Century modern lives. Anyone of us who can't receive His gentle guidance is *self-reliant.* And we too must, "discard" such idols "as filthy rags" and set our lives to living in and enjoying *"unbroken companionship"* with almighty God!

> *Blessed (happy, fortunate, to be envied) are all those who [earnestly] wait for Him, who **expect and look and long for Him** [for His victory, His favor, His love, His peace, His joy, and **His matchless, unbroken companionship**]!*
> (Isaiah 30:18 AMP)

Oral Roberts

So we need to wait on God more *[expecting, looking and longing for Him]*, by speaking and singing to Him more in tongues; communicating mysteries to God while building ourselves up in the Spirit and in faith at the same time.

It is times like this when we get so caught up in the spirit realm, that we can get visions and words from God. **When praying in this way we should seek the interpretation of what we are saying.**

This brings me to Oral Roberts. In his book called, **"Still Doing The Impossible,"** he confessed that after many years of ministry, especially the first 12 years, he had lacked decisiveness and direction! He even described himself as having been "wobbly spiritually" (Roberts 203).

In order to help us understand the specific role that *tongues and interpretation* played, especially in his earlier ministry, I have quoted several excerpts from the book, as follows: "I was full of ideas, some quite creative, but could not bring order and direction to them, or bring them to fruition… As the apostle Paul said, I was making an uncertain sound (1 Corinthians 13:1)" (Roberts 203).

Tongues and Interpretation

He went onto explain: "Something had to give, to change in me. This crisis brought me to the climactic choice of my life and ministry: to continue in this unsettled condition or to find the way I knew existed in God. *But how would I do it?* …I studied the nine gifts of the Spirit listed in first Corinthians 12:4-11" (Roberts 205).

"The gifts of tongues and interpretation of tongues fascinated me but I could not grasp them in a practical way… **I had no idea I could interpret back to my mind** (my understanding), God's response to my praying in the Spirit. I really did not know tongues is either praying in the Spirit or singing in the Spirit. I had not been taught much on this.

In a pivotal moment I learned how to pray in tongues at will and also interpret back to myself God's response…" (Roberts 206)

In short God told Oral Roberts to build a University. Of which Oral said, "I had no idea how to build a university…"

But God ignored this minor human limitation and gave Oral this instruction instead: "You are to build the university out of the same ingredient I used when I made the world - *nothing!*" (Roberts 206-207)

Receiving Revelation Knowledge

"I had no money, no buildings, no faculty, no students, no know-how, and few who believed I could accomplish this. I had never felt lonelier in my life. My mind was a blank sheet of paper... I burst into tears and fell to my knees in desperation" (Roberts 208).

He continued, "Suddenly a language from the Holy Spirit flowed up over my tongue. I had no idea what I was saying... I knew I was speaking mysteries. **I was invading that celestial realm where all true knowledge and wisdom reside.** It lasted only a minute or two. I rose to my feet, not knowing what to do next. Suddenly words in my own language began to pour forth from my mouth, **revealing knowledge I had been lacking... light from above flooded my mind. Suddenly I saw how to build God a university... I saw it... It was a crystal-clear vision. I had seen the invisible"** (Roberts 208).

Of this revelation knowledge Oral wrote: "In first Corinthians 14:13-15 Paul says we can use our will to pray in tongues and to interpret back to our understanding (mind). We receive God's revelation knowledge... **the revealing of God's Word by the Holy Spirit in ways you cannot find for yourself by studying the bible...** The Holy Spirit knows how to personalize what God is saying to you in His Word. To me this has been very important" (Roberts 209).

Oral stressed the following points however: "Revelation knowledge given to you must line up with the Word of God and be confirmed by it. It is not a jumping off in every direction or wild imagination. That can lead to forming a cult or joining one. **If revelation knowledge is not confirmed by the written Word of God, forget it**" (Roberts 209-210).

One Step at a Time

Someone once asked: "How do you eat an elephant?" The simple answer: "Just one bite at a time!"

Becoming overwhelmed in life is all too easy, especially in the ministry! The elephant illustrates that the only way to avoid becoming overwhelmed, is by taking simple steps and by making them one at a time.

As believers this first involves getting God's mind on the issue: "When God calls you to do something; you can give yourself wholly to Him and expect Him to equip you. He may not confirm this up front, but **as you take each step, more of His plan and His will, will be revealed to you**" (Roberts 210).

Have you ever heard the expression, *the devil's in the detail?* This simply means the small print often catches us out!

No matter how well we know our bibles, when it comes to the finer details of life, we must have that *view-from-the-trenches* advantage that only comes by God's ever-present Spirit with us. We must ever seek an un-broken connection with Him, especially when we find ourselves in the midst of life's unpredictable trials and circumstances.

So in this context, *tongues and interpretation* are so vital, as Oral explained above, because God supernaturally reveals life's small print: **"He helps us by revealing His Word by the Holy Spirit in ways we cannot find for ourselves as we study the bible."**

No Poetic Licence!

To have poetic licence means: *"license or liberty, esp. as taken by a poet or other writer, in deviating from conventional form, logic, fact, etc., to produce a desired effect. Freedom to deviate deliberately from normally applicable rules or practices (especially in behaviour or speech)."*

It should go without saying, that there is no such thing as *poetic licence* when it comes to the written Word of God! Nevertheless I will say it again, there's no room for reinterpretation of God's Word or any additional "special" revelations!

Although there is room for the genuine leading of the Holy Spirit, as author and indisputable inspiration of the bible! And we can recognise the Holy Spirit from other spirits, because He is the Spirit of Truth, and never leads us outside of the Word of God.

I have found in my own personal prayer life, that as I pray in tongues over the Word of God, relying on the Holy Spirit to reveal truth to my inner man, my spirit becomes more accessible to and enlightened by the truth.

God wants us to be enlightened and have the spirit of wisdom and revelation operating in our lives:

*That the God… may give unto you **the spirit of wisdom
and revelation in the knowledge of him: The eyes of
your understanding being enlightened…***
(Ephesians 1:17-18 KJV)

No time like the Present

This is a good place I believe, to encourage readers to
pray in tongues for at least 15 minutes (30 minutes or even
1 hour perhaps) a day! Like a ritual-mantra? NO! But as a
spiritual discipline, yes!

Let's quickly add here that any expression of our faith
devoid of relationship with the Holy Spirit - is dead works!

"Of course, discipline is a good thing **if it is inspired
by the Holy Spirit and flows from intimacy with Him.**
But discipline inspired by religious spirits will lead you to
put your trust in your own strength instead of His. Such
disciplines are powerless against the enemy, for they are
sponsored by evil spirits and will only lead to oppression in
our lives" (Vallotton 67).

Paul tells us in Ephesians 6:18 that we should pray in
the Spirit on _all_ occasions. **So we must practice speaking in
tongues as often as we can.**

This will help us develop and we will receive more
words. If we do not speak regularly in tongues, we will be
like little children babbling a few words.

We encourage our toddlers to say words over and over
again until they can speak them clearly. As they keep on, they
develop new words, likewise, tongues is a heavenly language

that we have to develop, we have to practice speaking them so that we will be clear and fluent.

While we are developing our tongues we will find that our prayer lives will become stronger and deeper. Tongues are the heavenly language and even though we might not know what we are praying, our spirits understand. Tongues is the tool our spirit uses to express itself to God when we do not know what to say in our own language.

An Unnatural Skill

Speaking in tongues is not a language that can be taught by someone or learned by reading a book, (you can't earn a PhD in tongues for example!) therefore cannot be reduced to human rationalisation.

God wants us to use our prayer language to the max, **not allowing ourselves to become crippled by fear** and doubt. He wants us to be free in every area of our lives. If we can take hold of our new tongues and realise the power and authority we have in Christ Jesus; Satan's influence in our lives will be reduced.

Satan wants us muzzled and in a spiritual-straight-jacket so that we no longer pose any threat to his plans. He rightly fears tongues and wants us to fear using them! So he dominates us by using our own fears against us!

However fear's influence can be radically diminished, but only if and when repelled by strong faith, "It is natural in people that when one senses fear in another, he will almost inevitably move to dominate that person. This is the very thing that the enemy of our souls does to us spiritually. Fear arouses demonic forces to swarm to the vulnerable. Likewise, faith repels them.

For this reason, it is a basic purpose of every Christian to walk in the faith that resists the enemy's attempts to dominate us. We then must grow in our dominion and faith for the purpose of serving others..." (Joyner, Breaking the Power of Evil 29-30)

Safeguards from Deception

Nevertheless there are clear guidelines that help keep error from the door of the Church. And while there is room to learn, if too much *flakiness* is left unchecked, it robs believers of the genuine experience and gifts that God gave to the Church.

Rodney Howard-Browne in his book called, **"Flowing in the Holy Spirit - A Practical Handbook on the Gifts of the Spirit"** wrote:

"The gift of divers kinds of tongues is a supernatural utterance in an unknown language. Someone may argue, *'I've been baptized in the Holy Spirit. I speak in tongues. So I've got one of the nine gifts.'* No you don't. I said, **No, you don't!**

Diverse kinds of tongues is _not_ your prayer language, and your prayer language is _not_ one of the nine gifts of the Spirit. Let me explain.

For one thing, divers tongues is not as *you* will; it's as the *Spirit* wills. That proves to me that divers kinds of tongues is not your prayer language, because you should be able to speak in tongues when *you* want to; but you can't give a message in divers kinds of tongues when you want to. It's only as the Spirit wills. Every one of the nine gifts of the Spirit is as the Spirit of God wills, not as you will.

Banana, Banana, Banana

This is an area where we're having problems in the churches today. People come to the mike and say something like, *'Banana, banana, banana,'* and they go sit down. They wait for the interpretation for *'banana,'* but there's not going to be any. Do you know why? Because it never was a 'message' in the first place! These people are simply speaking something out of their own private prayer language.

The bible says that when you pray in an unknown tongue, you speak mysteries unto God *(see 1 Corinthians 14:2)*. God doesn't want you to know what you're praying about! It's got nothing to do with you. That's why He gives you a private prayer language: so you won't interfere with what the Spirit of God is praying through you!

If half the Christians knew what they were praying by the Spirit of God, they would quit praying. They would say, *'I don't want* **that.**' Meanwhile, the Spirit of God is praying *the perfect will of God* for you!

To summarize, divers tongues is as *the Spirit* wills. Your prayer language is as *you* will. That's simple enough to understand...

We've got too many people getting up to give a message in tongues when it's not a message in tongues. **It's not divers tongues. It's their prayer language, and they should be told it is"** (Howard-Browne 43-44).

❖

CHAPTER 6

Beating the Air Aimlessly

By praying in tongues and being led of the Spirit, from our inner man, we too can be mighty against our enemies. With Him, we can continually *enforce* Christ's victory by faith and we too can be successful and anointed **warriors** *(not worriers)* for God!

I might add here to clarify my views on this subject that **we should not go looking around in the spirit world to see what we can attack!** I have seen many stumble due to this kind of foolish mentality. It's a fact that no military in the world (unless tyrannical or despotic), would go to war just for the sake of it.

War is the *last* resort for any sane government, as war is extremely *costly* in terms of the economy and human life expenditure. Civilised countries historically only go to war if and when threatened, principally to protect its own interests and those of its populace.

We are not Bounty Hunters

Clearly if we go looking for trouble - we'll find it! It does not do the Lord or us any favours chasing demons down for no good reason. We are not bounty hunters. That's not our job. Nowhere in scripture are we commissioned to do that.

In fact if we talk and think about demons more than we do God, or more than we worship, then there is definite deception with our theology! Moreover Jesus knew demons existed but He did not waste His time looking for them. He spent His time, *"doing good, and healing all that were oppressed of the devil; for God was with him" (Acts 10:38 KJV)*. His concerns were for *people **not** demons!* Besides, He did not need to go looking for demons; they often came looking for Him!

> *And the evil spirit answered and said, Jesus I know, and Paul I know; but who are ye?*
>
> *(Acts 19:15 KJV)*

We must understand that there are always ***consequences*** to spiritual warfare. It is essential to be led of the Holy Spirit – otherwise we will face such consequences alone!

> *Some itinerant Jewish exorcists who happened to be in town at the time tried their hand at what they assumed to be Paul's "game." They pronounced the name of the Master Jesus over victims of evil spirits, saying, **"I command you by the Jesus preached by Paul!"***

80

The Seven sons of a certain Sceva, a Jewish high priest, were trying to do this on a man when the evil spirit talked back: **"I know Jesus and I've heard of Paul, but who are you?"** *Then the possessed man went berserk – jumped the exorcists, beat them up, and tore off their clothes. Naked and bloody, they got away as best they could.*

(Acts 19:13-16 MSG)

Spiritual babies, who venture out alone into spiritual matters, don't have the capacity to deal with the backlash that is inevitably provoked. The Holy Spirit *empowers* us to do whatever *He* expects us to do - it goes without saying then, that *without* His initiative - we are powerless. It is my personal view, that it is not advisable to do *anything spiritual* without the Holy Spirit. He alone is the Spirit of truth. All else is deception. Simple.

Willing and Obedient

From his popular mini-book series of the mid-nineties, called **"The Holy Spirit"** Ulf Ekman wrote: "He cannot lead you until you are honestly willing to obey Him. Be totally available to Him, whatever He wants to do with you. The Holy Spirit is the Spirit of truth who convinces the world of sin, righteousness and judgment (John 16:8). He will show you exactly where you are spiritually, and **you will not move a step further until you agree with Him**" (Ekman, The Holy Spirit 23).

Some have mistakenly perceived that because they have authority in Christ – they can do as they please. Surely each individual who tries this route – eventually learns the hard way! Clearly it must repetitively be echoed that as believers our lives *must* actively be being led by the third person of the Trinity - **The Holy Spirit.**

"How do we get to know the Holy Spirit? We only become aware of His nature as we enter a life of prayer" (Cho 37).

Stay under Authority

No soldier goes to battle under his own authority. If he did he wouldn't last very long! David slew Goliath alone – yet he had God's backing and also King Saul's. He did not rush to sort out Goliath without first speaking to Saul who gave his blessing.

Even though his brothers ridiculed his youthful zeal – it was King Saul who took him seriously *(he had nothing to lose!)* And it was King Saul who had legitimate authority over David, regardless of his brother's opinions.

So David went out to stand before Goliath with the assurance that his *(heavenly)* God and his *(earthly)* king were backing him up! And it was to them that David submitted his fervent zeal and faith, but not to those who mocked him.

It's right then to wonder what might have happened that day had David not followed correct protocol *(it could have been a **very** different story!)* To which, it's important to add, that zeal alone is not enough to qualify *any* soldier. And as the above scripture in Acts chapter 19 highlights, evil spirits know exactly who we are and whether legitimate authority backs us up or not!

I believe that we need strategy and this can be found within the Body of Christ, by working together with the mature of the brethren. However Pastors, a word of caution – and that from experience - don't expect babies to be warriors! They will not be able to stand.

Remember also that God gives different anointings for different tasks within the Body. Yes everyone has the ability to lay hands on the sick and cast out demons, but not everyone is anointed to be a Goliath slayer. If we just gave the fivefold ministry some much-deserved credibility, then we would be able to recognise that sometimes it takes the likes of the apostolic and prophetic *(anointing)* to turn a city upside down!

If we want to see real change happen, then we must bring in some *anointed-gun-slinging-loud-preaching-challenging-prophetic-types;* the Holy Spirit will use them and for sure we'll witness authentic change in the atmosphere and the devil run out of town!

Fivefold Specialists

God has equipped, appointed and anointed the fivefold ministries for special tasks, which the average rank-and-file Christian soldier would not be able or have the capacity to handle. The fivefold minister has been trained at length to cope with events on another level! So we must allow them to do what they are trained and appointed to do.

Besides we did not commission them, God did and if we stifle them we will be keeping the *ceiling* of our spiritual growth subdued and low, *(by which event the general people*

83

will feel defeated, oppressed and discouraged). Inversely God has given the Body of Christ *everything* it needs to thrive and succeed, which *essentially* includes the fivefold ministry gifts.

If they pose a threat – it's only for the devil! And the challenge they provoke is necessary and conducive with the *change* we want. Remember nothing changes without challenge *(weight loss, fitness or muscle growth comes with much necessary resistance)* so we can't cry out for change and then monitor how God brings it – that's His business!

The Lord is a Warrior

So as we saw earlier, the bible tells us in Exodus 15:3 that our Lord is a Warrior, therefore as a warrior He understands strategy. The fivefold ministry is part of that strategy for spiritual warfare – which is more than tongues and involves not just praying but also anointed preaching to break open the atmosphere.

In and through all, God does not advocate that we wage war against people. The Old Testament involved one bloody battle from another. Not so with the New Covenant. The opposite is true. *People* are never our enemies, even though the devil can and does use them *(like Judas).*

But let there be no mistaking; yes we **do have enemies and still *must* wrestle, but NOT against people.** In as much that we wrestle against principalities and powers, against the kingdom of darkness. They operate on earth and in heavenly places, yet God furnished us with the supernatural weapons needed, to defeat them!

❖

CHAPTER 7

Warring Tongues

To inspire some balance on this subject of warring tongues, Jack Hayford shares: "A letter addressed to a friend of mine from Cfan *(Christ for all Nations)* Frankfurt June 28, 1991 said…"

"Concerning your question on warring tongues – you know, I would like to give you just some practical advice and that is: *Always follow what is in your inner man.* You read the whole situation perfectly right that this is just another strategy of the enemy to try and divert people from spiritual warfare – absolutely right.

Warring Tongues or Speaking Secrets

There is no such thing as warring tongues in the bible. Many people say that this is their experience and that they pray far more aggressively when they pray in tongues, which is all true and well. But that is God's prerogative. If He wants to use tongues in spiritual warfare against the devil, then that is His prerogative and it is not for me to decide against it or how and when to use it.

As far as my understanding of the Word of God goes, tongues has been given to us to speak secrets unto God and that is how it should stay. If God should decide to use that secret in spiritual warfare, that is something He decides and *if you come under that kind of flow in the Spirit, then do it.* But there is no way you could use that as a basis to teach from or to just simply say, *'Well, I just war in tongues against the devil.'* I trust this makes it very clear unto you...*yours Cfan."*

Another letter to a Pastor in the Midlands *(England)* who was searching for the truth on this subject wrote to Kenneth Hagin for clarification. In his reply dated 5th February 1991, he said,

"Regarding your letter, *(on warring tongues)* I am enclosing a copy of an article, which appeared in the Fall 1990 issue of *'The New Breed,'* which is a publication available only to alumni of RHEMA Bible Training Centre.

This article was written by the head of our alumni department and ministerial association, it reflects the viewpoint of this ministry concerning warring tongues and groaning. I trust it will help to clarify these matters for you... Yours in Christ, Kenneth E. Hagin."

A Balanced Perspective

Tony Cooke who was the head of Rhema's alumni department, shared some of his concerns:

"A teaching, which has surfaced recently and one that merits our attention is that of *'warring'* tongues and *'groaning.'* Proponents of this doctrine claim that this teaching is a higher revelation intended to take the believer into a deeper, more advanced realm of spiritual warfare.

But is this teaching and the practices it advocates leading saints in deeper spirituality, or is it leading believers into fleshly extremes and excesses? Having reviewed some of the teaching on this subject, I have seen several areas of concern, which include the following:

Several areas of Concern

Instead of emphasising the triumph of Jesus over Satan, the position of the believer in Christ, and the authority that is resident in the believer, this teaching portrays believers as being oppressed and defeated under the lordship of Satan.

The emphasis is not on what Christ has done, but rather the emphasis is on what the Christian must do in order to get victory *over* the devil. The believer is thereby instructed to *'groan'* and to *'war'* in tongues in order to obtain victory.

However, the bible teaches that Satan is already a defeated foe through the death, burial, and resurrection of Christ, and that in Christ every believer participates in Jesus' victory over Satan. This is not to deny that Christians must exercise their authority over Satan, but the error I think is one of focus and position. Correct biblical authority is exercised from a seated and victorious position in Christ in which the enemy is under our feet.

According to this doctrine, praying is not at all focused on fellowshipping with the Father God, but is predominantly oriented and fixed on *'battling the devil.'*

In other words, Satan, not God, becomes the focus of one's spiritual activities. But the Apostle Paul wrote that when the Christian speaks in tongues he is speaking mysteries unto God and is edifying himself *(1 Corinthians 14:2,4)*. This teaching, however, ignores this biblical emphasis and strives to make speaking in tongues something that is done against the devil instead of unto God.

Anyone who is offended at the shrieking, screaming, yelling and the other excesses, which occur and which this teaching encourages is labelled as having religious devils which need to be cast out.

The story of Jesus at the tomb of Lazarus *(John 11:38)* is used to substantiate their doctrine of groaning. Although the bible does say that Jesus did groan here, it should be noted that neither **Jesus nor Paul ever taught people how to groan or gave them** *'groaning lessons.'* The fact that John explicitly addressed Jesus' groaning in this manner would seem to indicate that this was not a normal ritual in Jesus' life, but rather, more of a unique occurrence.

The story of the Israelites groaning in the Book of Exodus is also used by the proponents of this teaching to prove that if you will groan, God will hear you and deliver you.

It should be noted that groaning of the Israelites in the Old Testament was the result of the torments of the Egyptian bondage and has no connection whatsoever with the Spirit of God moving upon a person in true intercession.

Also, the New Testament does not teach that God will deliver you if you groan long enough or loud enough. Rather, it teaches that through God's grace and the redemptive work of Jesus, God '...*HATH delivered us from the power from darkness, and hath translated us into the kingdom of his dear Son' (Colossians 1:13 KJV)*. Besides, the bible says that it pleases God *(Hebrews 11:6)*."

He concludes by Saying

"Finally **and most importantly** it should be noted that we need to deal with every issue such as this one as positively as possible lest we be found *'throwing the baby out with the bath water.'* We must avoid over reacting to error by neglecting and ignoring the true issues at hand.

For instance, the Church cannot afford to back away from valid intercession, true spiritual warfare, and spiritual groanings, which come as a result of the prompting of the Holy Spirit. We should and we *must* press into the genuine things of the Spirit and be fervent in prayer as the Scriptures teach.

There is a genuine intercession in which the Church must stir itself up to participate… There are indeed spiritual battles to be fought and won in prayer and there are true groanings that will come upon the believer at times as the *Spirit of God* moves upon him in that fashion. Yet we also must not be ignorant of doctrines and practices, which go beyond the Word of God and lead people into excess and error."

I included the article and letters above to enhance balance. Nonetheless the facts don't change, that Jesus *still* requires us to be His prayer warriors! God Himself is *still* a warrior *(Exodus 15:3)* and He *still* hates it when His people are attacked and has given us ***mighty spiritual weapons*** to demolish them with! *(Why else did God give us weapons, if He did not intend for us to use them?)*

> *For though we live in the world, we do not wage war as the world does.* ***The weapons we <u>fight</u> with*** *are not the weapons of the world. On the contrary, they* ***have divine power to demolish strongholds.***
>
> *We demolish arguments and every pretension that sets itself up against the knowledge of God, and we take captive every thought to make it obedient to Christ.*
> *(2 Corinthians 10:3-5)*

Look at what William Kumuyi, (the African co-ordinator for the AD 2000 Movement and a leader in the Spiritual Warfare Network) had to say about this precise point:

Taking Advantage of the Ignorant

"The enemy often takes advantage of our ignorance. If you are fighting an unseen enemy who is determined to destroy you and you are not vigilant, and you do not even know that there is a fight going on, the enemy will take advantage of that ignorance and defeat you in the middle of battle."

Therefore it's vital that we acknowledge there is still a war going on, and that God did not fail or neglect to equip us well for it. Even though Jesus won the ultimate war, there are still battles going on and we must fight to win! To which I add a tremendously valid point: GREATER THAN THE DANGER OF GLORIFYING THE ENEMY, IS TO BE IGNORANT OF THE ENEMY!

Praying from a place of Victory not Defeat

To further this point, that we must come from a place of VICTORY, I have taken an excerpt from Beni Johnson's book, "The Happy Intercessor."

"Football is an all-American pastime... On a football team you have a defensive team and an offensive team. The defensive team tries to steal the football from the opposing offensive team.

The defensive team will try to figure out the offensive team's strategies and plays. The offensive team, however, has the advantage in that they have the ball... The offensive team calls the plays, for they have the ball...

For intercessors, it is extremely important to understand that God has already given us the ball. We are the offensive team. If you don't understand that, if you are not praying from a place of victory, then you will be an intercessor whose prayer life is marked with defeat.

You will be one who is always trying to protect what God has given you from the devil's plans or, worse yet, running after the devil and trying to figure out what he is doing. How wrong is that? **If you do not understand that God has already given you the ball, you will live in fear and pray from a place of lack.**

When Joe Montana (…our favourite quarterback of all time) would throw that ball down the field, he knew right where it was going—right into the hands of his receiver. It was a thing of beauty.

What a picture for us of how to live as Kingdom people who know the plays of Heaven. A good player will be so focused on his target that it feels like there is no one else around. **A good player does not just throw the ball around. Similarly, we can't just throw our prayers around here and there.**

Like Joe, we are the offensive team. Offensive teams call the plays. They must have confidence that they are going to win. **They have to believe that they will win because they know that they control the ball.**

As intercessors, we need to always remember that we are playing on an offensive team. On an offensive team, the entire team knows where the ball will go and who will catch it. The entire team knows where to run.

Praying for the Touchdown

They have one focus: to get the touchdown. As intercessors, we must listen for the plays that the Lord is calling and pray them in so that the team can catch the ball and make the touchdown.

Our job is not to spend all of our time worrying about the enemy's strategies. We are to make the plays that God calls.

A lot of intercessors spend all of their time worrying about what the enemy will do next, but their job is to focus on God and to partner with His plans.

As an intercessor, your job is to find out what God wants to do, which is the opposite of what the enemy is saying. Then you begin to pray what God wants. **You don't allow the enemy to bring distraction. <u>You have to make a choice not to partner with fear</u>.**

This is how intercessors live an offensive lifestyle. They pray according to God's plans, and <u>they pray from a place of victory</u> [Ephesians 4:14]" (Johnson, Beni 52-55).

❖

CHAPTER 8

The Gift of Tongues

Going back to tongues: it must be established that tongues is a *gift* and has its origin in the Holy Spirit. He knows how to disarm the enemy. He is the Spirit of *"might and power"* *(not just feelings, goose bumps and whispers!)*

We must recognise that there are times, when we are praying in our prayer language, that God seemingly directs tongues and releases them through us like a weapon: right up from our inner-man comes loud, bold and strong tongues.

In 2 Corinthians 10:3, the bible tells us that we are in a spiritual war, anyone in a war needs the most powerful weapons, if one is to achieve victory. Likewise, we as the Body of Christ must use all that's available to us, to enforce the victory. We must also recognise that we have been given *"spiritual weapons"* for good reason!

Let's run through some things that can be constituted as being amongst our personal *arsenal* or *weaponry (used to resist oppression and the powers of darkness):*

- the Word of God *(using "it is written"),*

- the Holy Spirit *(the anointing that "breaks every yoke of bondage"),*

- faith *(that can move mountains),*

- prayer and intercession *(with tongues),*

- fasting,

- repentance *(brings effective personal progress),*

- the armour of God,

- the Name of Jesus,

- the blood of the Lamb,

- the word of our testimony *(by which we overcome),*

- prophecy,

- spiritual gifts,

- power *(grace)* and myriads of angels *("ministering spirits sent to minister to those who inherit salvation").*

Of course we could add much more to this list – but for the sake of space we're keeping it fairly short, still however it's easy to deduce that God's provision is substantial and weighty! We have certainly not been left abandoned to our own limited faith. In **no** way has our heavenly Father left us short. He is never *delinquent* or *negligent.* God has everything covered.

His Word a Creative Force

We must *activate* these weapons and realise that it's only with *spiritual-weapons* that we are going to win *spiritual battles;* the flesh cannot approach spiritual things. The devil knows this better than we do and triumphs exceedingly all the time he can successfully keep believers fixated in the natural realm *(or at best, limited in the spiritual realm!)* We pose no threat to him in the flesh. Only the spirit filled believers who know how to *operate* in the Spirit, pose the greatest threat to his kingdom.

So yes we have been given many weapons, however it is only by the power of the Holy Spirit, that *creative-force* can properly be given to them, particularly the Word. *(Note: praying the Word of God by the power of the Holy Spirit proves irresistibly potent!)*

> **It is by the Spirit of God that I drive out the demons...** *the kingdom of God has come upon you [before you expected it].*
>
> *(Matthew 12:28 AMP)*

> *So shall my word be that goeth forth out of my mouth:* **it shall not return unto me void, but it shall accomplish** *that which I please, and it shall prosper in the thing whereto I sent it.*
>
> *(Isaiah 55:11 KJV)*

The main way that we release our weapons is through prayer. Prayer is a launching pad for spiritual weapons! There are times when we pray in other tongues, that they flow from our inner man like a weapon, mighty against the forces of darkness. Flowing with great boldness and strength - with such volume - that can only be described as loud!

When we pray like this, the Holy Spirit releases God's power, will, plan and presence through us. It's notable to point out, that the presence of the Holy Spirit is the ONLY *restraining-force-against-evil* on this planet. Without Him – it would be hell-on-earth - with no conviction evil would easily reign and prevail and His light alone keeps the forces of darkness at bay.

> *And when he is come, he will reprove the world of **sin, and of righteousness, and of judgment.***
>
> *(John 16:8 KJV)*

> *But truly **I am full of power by the spirit of the LORD, and of judgment, and of might, to declare** unto Jacob his **transgression,** and to Israel his **sin.***
>
> *(Micah 3:8 KJV)*

Let the Light Shine

We therefore must ensure that the light keeps burning through us – by yielding to His presence and allowing Him to do what He wants to do through us. This is not done just by praying in tongues but by living a righteous life here on earth *(we create a conflict here on earth – just by living right before God in an evil atmosphere!)*

*For the kingdom of God is not meat and drink [flesh]; **but righteousness, and peace, and joy in the Holy Ghost.***
(Romans 14:17 KJV – emphasis ours)

*You prepare a table before me **in the presence of my enemies.** You **anoint** my head with oil; my [brimming] cup runs over.*
(Psalm 23:5 AMP)

Some people say, *"But how can you pray that way in other tongues? I thought tongues were just for speaking to God. Are you fighting God?"*

This can be simply answered by saying:

Tongues open the door to the supernatural. We operate in the spirit when we speak in tongues. With it we can speak <u>to</u> God, and with it we can also speak <u>before</u> God – as the Spirit directs.

Remember, we don't beat the air aimlessly,

*Therefore I do not run uncertainly – without definite aim. **I do not box as one beating the air and striking without an adversary.***
(1 Corinthians 9:26 AMP)

This may seem foreign to us, but it is not foreign or even strange to the Holy Spirit, who anointed and led Samson to deliver God's people from their enemies.

❖

CHAPTER 9

Clarification about Tongues

As believers we need to recognise that there is room for praying softly and sensitively but there is also room for praying boldly, loudly and fervently. (God might not be deaf but He is not a nervous-wreck either!)

Some people like to use the word *"militant"* in place of *"fervent"* when it comes to prayer. However we find that the scriptural description of prayer is mostly *"fervent"* or *"earnest."*

So, for the sake of argument and to avoid any misinterpretation, we're going to stick with *"fervent"* and *"earnest,"* in this particular chapter!

For example most people can readily accept that God is *"fervent"* and that even His love for us is *"fervent"* (boiling hot, *jealous even!)* However generally speaking, if we described God or His love as "militant," this would be suggestive of aggression and be far too negative for most people.

To reach for balance, I have chosen to quote Lester Sumrall at this point *(who was not a fan of emotionalism in the church!)* I agree that there is room for believers to be *militant,* as long as they use the right sense of the word.

No Summer Soldiers

In "No Summer Soldiers," the first chapter of his book called, "The Militant Church" - Lester Sumrall wrote: "In God's army, you cannot be just a summer soldier; **full-time service is required.** It comes with the territory. In the United States *military,* there is a place for short-time enlistees; **but God's service is not like that.**

God wants soldiers, who are in it for the duration, soldiers who make a lifetime commitment to Him. From the moment you say yes to Jesus, you are in His service until you die – unless you go AWOL or shirk your duty. Does that sound like a stiff sentence? It may, if you do not personally know the Commander-in-Chief.

Volunteers for service with the Lord will not find it to be just a holy huddle. Spiritual warfare is just as real as any shooting war on the earth. Soldiers without their armour or who don't use their weapons can get ambushed, wounded and even killed, just as in a natural battle. And today, perhaps more than at any other time in history, Satan's manoeuvres are escalating. One look at your daily paper should convince you of this.

Those who served in the *military* – regardless the branch of service – will tell you being in the armed service is serious business, even in peacetime. It's not games you play. From the moment you enter the army, navy, marines, or air force, you are a part of something that exacts a price. Discipline and strict obedience to orders are not only expected but also required.

As Christians, we use *military terms* quite glibly sometimes in our reference to the warfare of the Christian life. Yet, far too often there is little real *militancy*, little willingness to endure, and a noticeable lack of a conquering spirit.

We understand so little about the Lord's battle plans. Make no mistake, living the Christian life means engaging in warfare when you are doing it God's way! ...Paul in writing to young Timothy said, *'You therefore must endure hardship as a good soldier of Jesus Christ'* (2 Timothy 2:3 KJV).

Military men are trained and equipped to do battle against the enemy. Carrying that analogy over into **the need for** *militancy* **in God's army** – and keeping in mind what the apostle wrote – one is impressed with the fact that **we are not to play at being soldiers. We are to take the idea of active spiritual warfare seriously.**

The call for effective service carries with it an implied understanding that we are to do battle, using our weapons in advancing against the enemy. *This is not peacetime soldiering!* **We are to be soldiers who know the battle plan and are mobilized for action"** (Sumrall 7-9).

Conversely brother Kenneth E. Hagin wrote in his book "The Triumphant Church:"

The Triumphant Church

"There are some people today who are talking about the militant church. Among them there are those who say that the Church of the Lord Jesus Christ needs to fight devils in order to be successful. But **I'd rather talk about the triumphant Church because that's scriptural.** Jesus' triumph over Satan is every believer's triumph. And every believer can enjoy that triumph and victory if he will walk in the light of his inheritance in Christ.

Those who continually talk about the militant church are those who are always trying to fight the devil: 'We're waging war on the devil. It's going to be tough! We are in for a battle!'

People who talk like that all the time need the eyes of the understanding enlightened to see that **the battle has already been won by Jesus Christ.** Now they just need to **stand** in that victory" (Hagin, The Triumphant Church 168).

To continue, whether we consider ourselves to be *militant* or *fervently triumphant* as scripture calls it *(arguably the same thing!)* prayer is something we do to RELEASE God's power and to make it available. Prayer is a mighty responsibility but also a weapon to be used.

Prayer is also a key to reaching the lost. If believers would reach out to God in prayer and intercede, they would discover God's strength and the anointing power, which would change their lives and the lives of those they are trying to reach.

There are *many* battles to be fought and won in the spirit realm, through strong, bold and fervent *(militant)* intercession. Our prayers can literally "release" the power of God and release people from darkness, bringing them into the light.

> So Peter was kept in prison, but **fervent prayer** for him was **persistently** made to God by the church (assembly).
> (Acts 12:5 AMP)

Because of the persistent and fervent *(not passive)* prayers of the church, God sent an angel to *"release"* Peter. That same power is available to us, today!

"Every born-again believer has God's ability abiding in him in the person of Jesus Christ; yet few have ever learned to *release* that power. God is in you to the degree that His Word is in you. God and His Word are one..." (Capps 9)

A Fervent Heart

To continue, sometimes *(not always)* it's necessary for us to pray loudly! Of course we can be bold and fervent without a lot of *noise* or *fan-fare* being involved either. It all depends on the situation at hand. Take Hannah for instance, who prayed with *all* her heart – yet no sound was heard leaving her mouth! Still, she was unquestionably *fervent* in spirit, to the point that Eli assumed that she was *drunk!*

> As she kept praying to the Lord, Eli observed her mouth. Hannah was praying in her heart, and **her lips were moving but her voice was not heard.** Eli thought she was drunk... "I am a woman who is deeply troubled. I

have not been dinking... **I was pouring out my soul to the Lord...** *I have been praying here out of my* **great anguish and grief."**

(1 Samuel 1:12-16)

There was nothing *passive* about her praying either - even though she was totally *silent.* The expression she gave to her fervency was different perhaps – but was still effective. Her quietness was certainly not an expression of peace and harmony - quite the opposite! She was very *troubled.* She needed God to hear her and she needed a significant *breakthrough.*

"In prayer it is better to have a heart without words than words without a heart." - John Bunyan

Eli also misunderstood the situation from the surface of it, but once he realised her actions were not motivated by drunken folly, he decreed, *"Go in peace, and may the God of Israel grant you what you have asked of him" (verse 17).* We all know the result! Her prayer was indeed answered. But on this occasion it did not come through shouting. Yet her prayers were not passionless and God took her very seriously.

Influenced by a Heart-condition

I included this section particularly to help those who think that God is *only* involved with *"shouting"* or deaf and impervious to any requests that are not *yelled* at Him!

Everything is influenced by the heart-condition of the petitioner. For New Covenant believers, it is also all about being led of the Holy Spirit, who knows how to approach the throne of grace in times of need and how to get results – every time.

See it this way: God-knows-how-to-approach-God, which is precisely who the Holy Spirit is. *He is God.* So there are no more *hit-and-misses* with our praying when He leads us.

Going back to the situation with Peter. Even though it does not specifically say that the church prayed loudly for Peter – it does say *fervently* and *persistently.* Yet we can safely assume their prayers were *audible.* As the bible also teaches that if we are praying publically *(in a group setting)* that we are to do so in such a manner that others can comprehend what we are praying and so can say "Amen!"

Hannah was different in that she was praying *alone.* She was not praying a prayer of agreement and was not looking for anyone to say *amen* with her! However when the church was praying for Peter, they were gathered "together." To agree with one another they would have been savvy to what each other was praying. Evidently the Holy Spirit was leading their prayers. We know this simply by its effectiveness!

So Hannah did not have any concerns about agreement. She was praying alone with God *(and eventually Eli)* who agreed with her! It was a different type of prayer.

So no ritual or doctrine need ever be made out of silent or audible praying – evidently there is room for both – as long as they are both fervent and faith filled!

So while some *(fervent)* prayers are quiet, others are accompanied with a shout, which is a usual demonstration or manifestation of boldness. However I am pressed to re-emphasise, that loud noise is NOT *always* synonymous with or equal to fervency, strength or boldness *(nor is it automatically excluded either!)*

Archbishop Desmond Tutu once said of conflict resolution: "Don't raise your voice, improve your argument."

What a great perspective! Yet still, I would rather say this: "Be carful to always be led of God's Spirit, Who knows exactly what each individual situation requires and in all realms!"

❖

CHAPTER 10

A Result of Faith

The problems only begin for us, when we assume that there is only *"one"* way or expression for doing something. That's when we miss it. *"Our church does it like this…"* *"Well 'our' church does it like that!"* We must simply be willing to flow by the Spirit however *He* wants to express Himself - through us in prayer (Romans 8:26-28).

For instance on more than one occasion Jesus **"cried out in a <u>loud voice</u>"** *(John 7:37; John 11:43)*. Even His behaviour was bolder at times, than at others *(and was never recorded as being timid or lacking in confidence!)* He overthrew the tables of the moneychangers in the temple courts for instance, which was not a daily temperament for Jesus.

But when it did happen, no one would ever forget it either! On this occasion Jesus was NOT *out-of-control* but *taking-back-control* of His *"Father's House"* (*Matthew* 21:12; *John* 2:14-17). His righteous indignation was on display, *"Zeal for your house will consume me"* (*John* 2:17). He *even* made a whip!

Furthermore, whenever there were times of making declarations in the bible – those declarations were rarely whispered! So while there are times when it's right to whisper – by faith – on other occasions the Holy Spirit will require a SHOUT or even a ROAR from the inside of us!

Faith has all kinds of expressions – but it is essential that the Spirit leads such *expressions,* so that they're not just fleshly out-bursts of *"free-expression!"*

> **Because of FAITH** the walls of Jericho fell down after they had been encompassed for seven days [by the Israelites].
> (Hebrews 11:30 AMP)

It was **"because of FAITH"** that the walls of Jericho fell. Taken personally this can apply to every obstacle in our lives, which need to be *"encompassed"* and *toppled (NOT by our shout but)* by our faith. But if there is faith in the shout and the Holy Spirit is leading – the result will always be victory, *(the flesh by itself can only produce noise and headache!)*

Sadly some people *only* know how to shout! They don't know that God is *also* in the *"still, small voice."*

> *After the earthquake a fire, but the Lord was not in the fire; and after the fire* **[a sound of gentle stillness and] a still, small voice.**
> (1 Kings 19:12 AMP)

We must *only* pray LOUD when the Spirit leads, so long as we understand there is more than one expression that the Holy Spirit uses to help us communicate and *"target"* our faith.

It seems funny now but I used to preach in a certain church, some years ago. And each time I visited that particular church, I became more and more convinced that they *really* believed, if their sound system wasn't wacked-up-till-breaking-point *(or till everyone was half deaf)* God couldn't hear them!

I would leave that place each time with a blistering headache *(that would last on average for two days post-meeting!)* It used to be so loud that, I still don't know to this day, how all those young babies could cope with the noise.

It was such an effort for me to remain sensitive to the Holy Spirit in the midst of all that noise. And there was no clear reason why everything they did just *had* to be so very loud.

So without labouring the point any further, there is more to faith than just noise. The same way we don't go around shouting all the time: at the grocers, gas station or school. There must be time to be sensitive. Even with Jericho's legitimate "shout" – there were still seven days of complete silence that preceded it! So let's reach for the balance in everything, because there's always the extreme.

Tremendous Power Available

We must conclude by saying, when it's time to shout let's SHOUT! *("**Shout** for joy to the Lord, all the earth... Make* *a joyful **noise** to the Lord" Psalm 100:1 NIV/AMP).* And when it's time to be quiet, sensitive and still then let's make sure we do that correctly too!

One thing is for certain; the enemy is greatly threatened when we begin praying fervently. James 5:16b clearly gives the answer why: *"The earnest (heartfelt, continued) prayer of a righteous man **makes tremendous power available** [dynamic in its working]" (AMP).*

Satan tries to hinder our *earnestness* and our *fervency* chiefly by getting us all hung-up-in-knots about **methods.** We must resist such restrictions on our prayers, knowing that our prayers are meant to be much more than just *wimpy* efforts!

"The church is looking for better methods; God is looking for better men. The Holy Ghost does not flow through methods, but through men. He does not come on machinery, but on men. He does not anoint plans, but men..." – E.M Bounds

Faith might seem *aggressive* sometimes because there is such a lot at stake - much to gain and much to lose. No parent would passively watch as his or her child was molested or abducted. No way! So there is ample room for aggression, **so long as it is fuelled by faith and love - not hatred or some other negative emotion.**

Everything we do, in fact must be done by faith, *"without faith it is impossible to please God" (Hebrews 11:6).* So whether we are shouting or whispering – we must always be led of the Spirit and be in faith. Without Him *anything* we do is just *dead* noise – regardless whether it's loud or not.

All our praying should be victorious. We are winners not losers. We are the head and not the tail. We are more than conquerors and we should NEVER just idly watch while the thief and destroyer tries to take our goods. The one who comes to *"steel, kill and destroy"* can only be stopped by the Holy Spirit in us who knows how to pray effectively.

Never Lacking in Zeal

So fervency is very important for effective intercession. We should always be fervent when we pray. In fact the bible teaches that we are ALWAYS to be *"fervent in spirit" (Romans 12:11 KJV)*.

NEVER *lag in zeal and in earnest endeavour;* be aglow and *burning with the Spirit,* serving the Lord.
(Romans 12:11 AMP)

NEVER *be lacking in zeal,* but keep your *spiritual fervour,* serving the Lord.
(Romans 12:11)

W.E. Vine says: The word translated *"fervent"* in Romans 12:11 means, **"to be HOT or to BOIL."** The Strong's Concordance adds that figuratively it means, *"to be earnest."* Epaphras was *"labouring fervently"* for the Colossians in prayers *(Colossians 4:12)*. The Greek word AGONIZOMAI translated *"labouring fervently"* indicates **a striving and a wrestling.** Ephesians 6:12 is a part of this struggle.

For we are not wrestling with flesh and blood [contending only with physical opponents], but against the despotisms, against the powers, against [the master

*spirits who are] the world rulers of this present darkness,
against the **spirit forces of wickedness in the heavenly
(supernatural) sphere.***

(Ephesians 6:12 AMP)

The best defence is offence. Why? Because through Jesus
Christ we already have the victory! However this does not
mean that we can afford to sit back and relax, by no means
*(in fact the victory we have in Christ must be constantly enforced
and never taken for granted).* As believers, we MUST be fervent
and watchful *"Be on your guard [constantly alert], and watch
and pray..." (Mark 13:33; Mark 14:38 AMP)*

Praying at ALL TIMES

Pray at all times *(on every occasion, in every season)* ***in
the Spirit,*** *with* ***all [manner of] prayer*** *and entreaty.
To that end* ***keep alert and watch with strong purpose
and perseverance,*** *interceding in behalf of all the saints
(God's consecrated people).*

(Ephesians 6:18 AMP)

Ephesians 6:18 is a loaded verse of scripture. There is just
so much in it. It could preach all by itself! But right where
it says, *"Pray at all times... with ALL manner of prayer and
entreaty"* this does include praying in tongues. There is no
doubting it; *"tongues"* have a vital role to play in our prayer
lives – that's why they are aptly described as our *"prayer
language."*

❖

Bibliography

- Bounds, E.M. <u>The Complete Works of E.M Bounds on Prayer</u>. Copyright © 1990. Published by Baker Book House Company. Printed in USA.

- Capps, Charles. <u>Releasing the Ability of God through Prayer</u>. Copyright © 1978. Published by Harrison House, Inc. Printed in USA.

- Cho, Paul Y. <u>Prayer: Key to Revival</u>. Copyright © 1984. Published by Word Books Publisher. Printed in USA.

- Ekman, Ulf. <u>A Life of Victory</u>. Copyright © 1991. Published by Word of Life Publications. Printed in Sweden.

- Ekman, Ulf. <u>The Church of the Living God</u>. Copyright © 1994. Published by Word of Life Publications. Printed in Sweden.

- Ekman, Ulf. <u>The Holy Spirit</u>. Copyright © 1995. Published by Word of Life Publications. Printed in Sweden.

- Goff, James R. <u>Fields White Unto Harvest</u>. Copyright © 1988. Published by University of Arkansas Press. Printed in USA.

- Hagin, Kenneth E. <u>The Triumphant Church</u>. Copyright © 1995. Published by Faith Library Publications. Printed in USA.

- Hagin, Kenneth E. <u>Why Tongues</u>. Copyright © 1975. Published by Faith Library Publications. Printed in USA.

- Hayford, Jack. Prayer is Invading the Impossible. Copyright © 2002. Published by Bridge-Logos Publishing. Printed in USA.

- Hinn, Benny. Good Morning Holy Spirit. Copyright © 1990. Published by Thomas Nelson, Inc. Printed in USA.

- Howard-Browne, Rodney M. Flowing in the Holy Spirit. Copyright © 2000. Published by Destiny Image Publishers Inc. Printed in USA.

- Johnson, Beni. The Happy Intercessor. Copyright © 2009 iBook. Published by Destiny Image ® Publishers, Inc. USA.

- Johnson, Bill. Strengthen Yourself in The Lord. Copyright © 2007. Published by Destiny Image ® Publishers, Inc. Printed in USA.

- Johnson, Bill. The Supernatural Power of a Transformed Mind. Copyright © 2014. Published by Destiny Image ® Publishers, Inc. Printed in USA.

- Joyner, Rick. Breaking the Power of Evil. Copyright © 2008. Published by Destiny Image ® Publishers, Inc. Printed in USA.

- Joyner, Rick. Overcoming Evil in the Last Days. Copyright © 2009. Published by Destiny Image ® Publishers, Inc. Printed in USA.

- Moore, Beth. Breaking Free: Discover the Victory of Total Surrender. Copyright © 2007. Published by B&H Publishing Group. Printed in USA.

- Murray, Andrew. The Believer's Prayer Life, A Classic on Prayer. Copyright © 1983. Published by Bethany House Publishers. Printed in USA.

- Parham, Mrs Charles. The Life of Charles F. Parham. Copyright © 1930. Published by Commercial Printing Company. Printed in USA.

- Roberts, Oral. Still Doing the Impossible. Copyright © 2002. Published by Destiny Image ® Publishers, Inc. Printed in USA.

- Silk, Danny. Keep Your Love On. Copyright © 2013. Published by Red Arrow Media. Printed in USA.

- Stone, Perry. The Code of the Holy Spirit. Copyright © 2013. Published by Charisma Books. Printed in USA.

Bibliography

- Sumrall, Lester. <u>The Militant Church</u>. Copyright © 1990. Published by Harrison House, Inc. Printed in USA.

- Vallotton, Kris. <u>Spirit Wars</u>. Copyright © 2011 Ebook edition. Published by Chosen Books USA.

- Strong, James. S.T.D., L.L.D. 1890. <u>Strong's Exhaustive Concordance; Dictionaries of the Hebrew and Greek Words</u>. e-Sword ® version 7.6.1 Copyright © 2000-2005. All Rights Reserved. Registered trade mark of Rick Meyers. Equipping Ministries Foundation. USA www.e-sword.net.

- Unless otherwise indicated, all scriptural quotations are from the HOLY BIBLE, NEW INTERNATIONAL VERSION ®. NIV ®. Copyright © 1973, 1978, 1984 by the International Bible Society. Used by permission of Zondervan Publishing House. All rights reserved.

- Scripture quotations marked AMP are taken from The Amplified Bible. Old Testament copyright © 1965, 1987 by Zondervan Corporation, Grand Rapids, Michigan. New Testament copyright © 1958, 1987 by The Lockman Foundation, La Habra, California. All rights reserved.

- Scripture references marked KJV are taken from the King James Version of the Bible.

- Scripture references marked MSG are taken from The Message. Copyright © 1993, 1994, 1995, 1996, 2000, 2001, 2002. Used by permission of NavPress Publishing Group.

- Scripture references marked NASB are taken from the NEW AMERICAN STANDARD BIBLE®, Copyright © 1960,1962, 1963,1968,1971,1972,1973,1975,1977,1995 by The Lockman Foundation. Used by permission.

- Scripture references marked NKJV are taken from the New King James Version. Copyright © 1982 by Thomas Nelson, 1982 by Thomas Nelson, Inc. Used by permission. All rights reserved.

- Scripture references marked VOICE are taken from The Voice™. Copyright © 2008 by Ecclesia Bible Society. Used by permission. All rights reserved.

❖

Ministry Profile

Doctor Alan Pateman, an apostle, is the President and Founder of **"Alan Pateman Ministries International"** (APMI), which was established in England back in 1987, a Christian-based *(parachurch)* non-profit and non-denominational outreach. This ministry is now focusing in two main areas: First **"Connecting for Excellence"** Apostolic Networking (CFE) and secondly, the teaching arm, **"LifeStyle International Christian University"** (LICU).

CFE is a multi-facetted missions organisation with the purpose of connecting leaders for divine opportunities and building lasting relationships, to touch the lives of leaders literally the world over. Apostle Dr Alan Pateman has to date ordained more than 500 ministers in over 50 NATIONS. In addition there are ministries, churches and schools who are in Association or Affiliation, looking to him for apostolic counsel and oversight.

Secondly LICU, which was founded in 2007, is a study program to help people discover their purpose and destiny. A global network of university campuses and correspondence students, demonstrating the Supernatural Kingdom of God through Doctrinal, Apostolic and Prophetic Teaching. Dr Alan holds the position of President/CEO, Professor of Theology, Biblical Studies and Apostolic Ministry. LICU is exploding throughout Europe, Asia and Africa, enhancing the Body of Christ

Dr Alan has authored more than 35 books including numerous teaching materials and LICU university courses (30) along with hundreds of Truth for the Journey articles on kingdom lifestyle *(that are regularly distributed globally via the internet).*

He is recognised as an Apostle, Bishop, Leadership Mentor, University Educator, Motivational Speaker, Connector and Author, who has also been featured on national and international TV and radio networks throughout the years.

Currently Apostle Alan, his wife Dr Jennifer reside in Lucca *(Tuscany)* Italy and travel out from their Apostolic Company.

- Alan Pateman Ph.D., D.Min., D.D., M.A., B.Th.

Academic Background

Dr. Alan Pateman attended several colleges throughout his training *(including studying Theology at Roffey Place, Horsham, UK and a Member of Kerygma - with Rev. Colin Urquhart and Dr. Bob Gordon - 1985-1987)* before being awarded a Doctorate of Divinity *(2006)* in recognition of his lifetime achievements by the International College of Excellence, now "DanEl Christian College" *(President: Dr. Robb Thompson USA)* also "Life Christian University" *(Dr. Douglas Wingate USA)* where he also earned a Bachelor of Theology B.Th. *(2006)*, a Master of Arts in Theology M.A., a Doctor of Ministry in Theology D.Min., *(2007)* and Doctor of Philosophy in Theology Ph.D. *(2013)* from LICU.

❖

To Contact the Author

Please email:

Alan Pateman Ministries International

Email: apostledr@alanpateman.com
Web: www.AlanPatemanMinistries.com

*Please include your prayer requests
and comments when you write.*

❖

Other Books

Media, Spiritual Gateway

Let's face it; we live in the era of fake news! It's always existed, but never been quite so prominent. Today it's an all-out-war between fact and political fiction.

ISBN: 978-1-909132-54-2, Pages: 192, Format: Paperback, Published: 2018 *Also available in eBook format!*

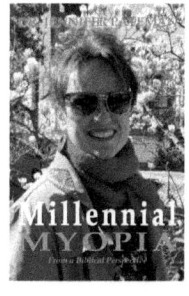

Millennial Myopia, From a Biblical Perspective

The standard for every generation is Jesus. However Millennial Myopia describes the trap of focusing everything on one particular generation or demographic cohort, at the exclusion and expense of all others. The Church cannot afford to make this mistake too.

ISBN: 978-1-909132-67-2, Pages: 216, Format: Paperback, Published: 2017 *Also available in eBook format!*

Truth for the Journey Books

WINNING by Mastering your Mind

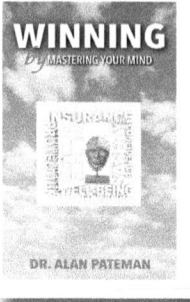

Someone once said, "Happiness begins between your ears and your mind is the drawing room for tomorrow's circumstances..." Remember, what happens in your mind will happen in time, and therefore one of our first priorities must be mind-management.

ISBN: 978-1-909132-40-5, Pages: 136,
Format: Paperback, Published: 2017
Also available in eBook format!

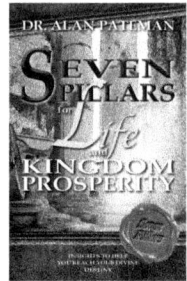

Seven Pillars for Life and Kingdom Prosperity

I submit these "Seven Pillars for Life and Kingdom Prosperity" to you, (Love, Prayer, Righteousness, Obedience, Connections, Management, Money). It's my desire that you walk in the triumphs that God has ordained for you.

ISBN: 978-1-909132-46-7, Pages: 220,
Format: Paperback, Published: 2016
Also available in eBook format!

Seduction & Control:
Infiltrating Society & the Church

This book is a glance into the world of seduction and control, how they try to influence the Church through many powerful avenues such as the New Age, sexual education in our schools, basic entertainment; things that touch our everyday lives in order that we effectively and gradually become desensitised.

ISBN: 978-1-909132-00-9, Pages: 156
Format: Paperback, Published: 2015
Also available in eBook format!

Truth for the Journey Books

Kingdom Management for Anointed Prosperity

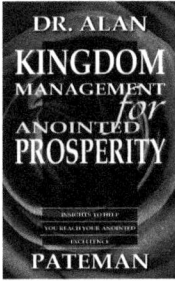

In his book, "Kingdom Management for Anointed Prosperity," Dr. Alan Pateman reveals how we can avoid living in continual crisis due to mismanagement. Life happens to all of us, but how we handle it matters most.

ISBN: 978-1-909132-34-4, Pages: 144, Format: Paperback, Published: 2015
Also available in eBook format!

Why War: A Biblical Approach to the Armour of God and Spiritual Warfare

Spiritual warfare means different things to different people, but from a biblical standpoint Ephesians 6:10-18 gives us the best biblical definition of spiritual warfare possible. We can also see how God has thoroughly equipped us for victory not just self defence!

ISBN: 978-1-909132-39-9, Pages: 180, Format: Paperback, Published: 2013
Also available in eBook format!

Forgiveness, The Key to Revival

Scripture is absolute when it comes to forgiveness. IF we forgive, THEN we are forgiven. It's that simple but no one said it was easy! Nonetheless, forgiveness can be likened to a spiritual key that unlocks spiritual doors and opportunities!

ISBN: 978-1-909132-41-2, Pages: 124, Format: Paperback, Published: 2013
Also available in eBook format!

Truth for the Journey Books

Revival Fires - Anointed Generals
Past & Present (Part Two of Four)

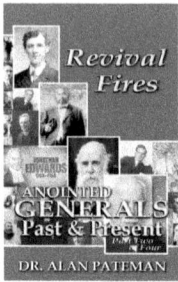

Seasons might be changing but God's Word remains the same. The heart of the author is to help train, equip and be a blessing to those men and women who will be willing to fulfil their potential in ministry and be properly equipped for service.

ISBN: 978-1-909132-36-8, Pages: 142,
Format: Paperback, Published: 2012
Also available in eBook format!

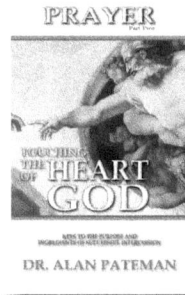

Prayer, Touching the Heart of God (Part Two)

Touching the Heart of God is the very essence of prayer. Whether we are petitioning God with very specific requests or consecrating ourselves before Him and rededicating our lives - whatever the case may be – the true essence of all praying is "Touching the Heart of God."

ISBN: 978-1-909132-12-2, Pages: 180,
Format: Paperback, Published: 2012
Also available in eBook format!

Prayer, Ingredients for Successful Intercession
(Part One)

This Book is the first of two books on Prayer. Dr. Pateman provides an exhaustive study, showcasing the vital ingredients necessary for all successful prayer. An excellent power-packed teaching tool, either for the individual or for the local church prayer group, that's eager to lay a solid foundation but don't know where to start!

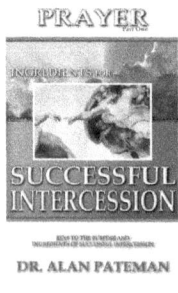

ISBN: 978-1-909132-11-5, Pages: 140,
Format: Paperback, Published: 2012
Also available in eBook format!

Apostles: Can the Church Survive Without Them?

Before Jesus returns a significant increase of the anointing will be poured out on the Body of Christ, but can the Church handle such an anointing? *(Acts 5:5)* Billy Brim once said, "As much as the anointing is powerful to create, it is as powerfully destructive of evil." The fear of God will be restored with the apostolic and people will begin walking with such anointing, as we have never seen before!

ISBN: 978-1-909132-04-7, Pages: 164, Format: Paperback, Published: 2012
Also available in eBook format!

Sexual Madness: In a Sexually Confused World

This book discusses the sensitive subject of political correctness in our world today and the growing fear of causing offence in the public arena. It also discusses the rise of homosexuality, pedophilia and all other forms of sexuality, as there are many. Including modern statistics on pornography.

ISBN: 978-1-909132-02-3, Pages: 160, Format: Paperback, Published: 2012
Also available in eBook format!

His Life is in the Blood

Blood is the trophy of every battle. The spilt blood of Jesus Christ is our trophy. It is our freedom from sin and bondage. Nothing can enter the blood-bought temples of the Holy Ghost! This book will encourage you to apply the blood of Jesus our Passover Lamb to your life, just as the children of Israel did in the Old Testament. Not merely talking or reading about it, but applying it.

ISBN: 978-1-909132-06-1, Pages: 152, Format: Paperback, First Published: 2007
Also available in eBook format!

LIFESTYLE UNIVERSITY | Raising Up Christian Leaders

Dear Friends,

Have you considered becoming one of our international students? We are privileged to welcome you, from around the world, to "LifeStyle International Christian University" *(the teaching arm of Alan Pateman Ministries International).* **An English speaking university** dedicated to your success; to see you trained and equipped to fully succeed in your God given Destiny.

It is our passion to raise up the leaders of tomorrow, who will have influence in all realms of authority, including the Body of Christ. Men and women of strategy, wisdom and true godliness, who'll stand with stature and maturity in this hour.

It's undeniable that in today's world, recognised education has become indispensable, therefore it is our desire to offer well balanced and well structured courses. Those that have been written by gifted and talented ministers of God, who seek to be inspired by God's Holy Spirit.

Consequently we have put together a **flexible curriculum,** designed both for correspondence students and campuses, which is a strategy to reach the distant learner; whether provincial, national or international. In fact we have many correspondence students from around the world, including a growing number of successful campuses, in various countries.

This is a growing platform, where men and women of dignity and passion, can grow and be established in their God given endeavours. As God is the healer of the nations, we pray and believe that many of our alumni will go on to **become world changers** in their own right.

We are proud of each and every one of our LICU students.

It would be our pleasure if you would join them on this incredible journey!

Doctor Alan Pateman

Alan Pateman Prof. Ph.D., D.Min., D.D., M.A., B.Th.
PRESIDENT AND CEO
www.licuuniversity.com www.cfeapostolicnetwork.com
Email: info@licuuniversity.com Mob: +39 366 329 1315

For more information visit our website/facebook or contact our office, using the details below:

Website: www.licuuniversity.com
Facebook: www.facebook.com/LICUMainCampus
Email: info@licuuniversity.com
Telephone: +39 366 329 1315

Alan Pateman Ministries
Presents

Conference

CONNECTING FOR
EXCELLENCE Lucca Italy

An international apostolic
and prophetic network

YOUR HOSTS: ALAN PATEMAN   JENNIFER PATEMAN

apostledr@alanpateman.com, Tel. 0039 366 329 1315
WWW.ALANPATEMANMINISTRIES.COM

Please contact our office or download the registration form.

Registration fee: €40

All Books Available

at

APMI PUBLICATIONS

Email: publications@alanpateman.com
*Also Available from Amazon.com
and other retail outlets.*

*If you purchased this book through Amazon.com
or other and enjoyed reading it, or perhaps one of
my other books, I would be grateful if you could
take a couple of minutes to write a Customer
Review, many thanks.*

www.ingramcontent.com/pod-product-compliance
Lightning Source LLC
Chambersburg PA
CBHW071550040426
42452CB00008B/1128